31 DIMES FROM HEAVEN

The secrets I learned from my Near-Death Experience

SARA MCCLELLAN

STOKE Publishing

Editing by Joanne Bell
ISBN: 978-1-988675-33-6

DISCLAIMER: I have tried to recreate events, locales and conversations from my
memories of them. In order to maintain their anonymity in some instances I have
changed the names of individuals and places, I may have changed some identifying
characteristics and details such as physical properties, occupations and places of
residence. This memoir was not written to cause harm or malice to any person or
family member. The book was written to share my spiritual journey of healing.

Dedication

This past year I lost five friends too early in their years. It was painful to see where some of them were in their lives. There was so much more for them to live. After the fifth, I made a deal with myself that I <u>would</u> sit down and write this book. I thought, Did they fill their purpose on this earth?
Thank you for reminding me life is precious.
To my girls who supported me at times when I was more like a child than a parent. Both of them beautiful girls, with gracious hearts. Thank you for loving me.
To my dear friends, Bob, Jim 1, Jim 2, and Shelly, Sharla, Laura, Will, Mel, Audrey, Trisha, Sandra, Dan, Trent, Peter, Loraine, Don and all the rest.
Thanking each of you for your love and support.
I want to thank Chantelle Adams for her "Shine Live" 2016 and Tiffany Carmouche for motivating me to write my book. I also thank Alicia Dunams for her "Write a Best Seller in a Weekend" and helping me face my fear of writing.
Last but not least to my dear late friend Juanita who was there for me so many times on my journey, sharing my tears and pain. Thank you for looking over me.
This year I began with a New Years resolution, To make my hard life matter.
Thank you for helping me with that!

Contents

Praise for 31 Dimes from Heaven

Sara McClellan had gone to the heart of healing and inspiration by sharing her story with us. Raw, emotional, gripping and uplifting, she follows a beautiful arc leading from pain, to an awakening, to healing and moving forward. Sara's book will help you reconnect with your intuition, signs of hope, and love that are all around you.

-Joanna Bell B.A., BMus., B. Ed. Educator, Editor,
Owner of Listoe-Bell Productions

Preface

In my late twenties I went through a Near-Death experience. I became completely connected with my soul again.

In that process discovered I was living in a very abusive environment all of my life. I didn't understand or remember that I had been severely abused as a child until I had a flashback of the abuse. This book is a twenty-year journey of how I healed the deepest wounds of my childhood through relationships, events, processes and techniques. I share the wisdom I received during the near-death and how that wisdom helped me heal my emotional damage.

In the beginning, writing this book was very emotional for me. I started the process of writing to help the reader, not realizing I was holding on to wounds that I needed to release. The peace I live in now brings me tears of joy. It is important to me that I have been very real and transparent to give depth to this story and to help my readers understand the wisdom I am sharing.

There were many people who influenced my healing process. The most influential were the late Wayne Dyer, Tony Robins, Oprah, Maya Angelou, Louie Schwartzberg, Michael Beckwith, Joel Osteen and Louise Hay. I also thank everyone along my path. Mr. G. Saunders and Mrs. C who reached out to me in my darkness with compassion. I am grateful for all the relationships along my journey that reflected back to me my inner beliefs – I was able to heal wounds through those mirrors. I thank my parents because I would not have a book to write if they were not exactly who they were as parents.

When you read this book please remember that I only had three memories of my childhood for more than thirty years of my life. The memories began to come back after I had a flashback of childhood abuse and my Near-Death experience. I then discover that I had blocked all my memories that were associated with the emotional pain. Most of my childhood.

My writing in the beginning of the book is the way I remember my childhood. I was numb and not able to feel depth. I tried my best to describe what I was going through to the best of my ability. As the book proceeds the writing becomes more detailed.

This book is very raw, vulnerable and intimate. I believe these qualities are needed to be able to reach the level of truth that we are all seeking.

May my words land
on hearts that need them!

ONE

Sneaky, Secret, Slithering Snake

TO THE OUTSIDE WORLD, we were the perfect family. The world thought my parents had the perfect marriage; fun-loving and carefree. I was the middle of three daughters and we were taught manners for eating in fancy restaurants, respecting elders, keeping quiet – learning what mattered to my parents to make us look good to the world. The kids in the neighbourhood thought my dad was the greatest. He played games like Champ with us and he was charming.

My parents would have lavish bridge parties, with cartons of cigarettes, lots of booze and lots of noise. I remember waking up in the middle of the night, after I had gone to sleep, to smoke wafting over my bed, loud noises and laughing.

When we were alone at home as a family, it was a very different story.

My dad, he was a sneaky snake. Slithering around at night, sneaking into my bedroom and violating me. Dirty, ugly secret, enough to make you shiver. Forcing me to live in a dark hole, hidden, shut completely down.

I was three years old when it started and I didn't have the words. I lived thirty-five years of my life before I could recall much of the first eleven years of my childhood – these three memories were all I had.

I was lying on my dad's chest, at three years old. He had a red plaid flannel shirt on. I felt the softness of his shirt on my cheek and the warmth of his body. I could hear his heart beating which was so comforting to me. His deep strong voice rumbled through his chest when he spoke to my mother. He had his strong arm around me and I felt as if nothing in the world could harm me.

The next memory I had was of lying in my bed and my mom was sitting on the side of the bed. I was upset, trying to tell my mom that something was wrong. I didn't have the words to explain what was wrong. I kept telling her my stomach hurt. As I was telling her, my dad walked past the door with this dark presence, and he said, "Stop being so melodramatic." I had no idea what that meant, but the way he said "melodramatic" in an angry dark tone, I decided it must be bad. In that moment, my world lost all its colour and became grey.

The third memory was the eclipse of the sun. I was playing on the swing set outside. My dad told me that if I looked up at the sun during the eclipse I would go blind. I was terrified.

I acted out by lying, stealing and sneaking around. I stole from my mom's purse, friends or whoever I could to feel better. I medicated with food, cookies, candy and TV shows.

My dad nicknamed me "George." I hated it. I was the boy in the family. Raised to build projects with my dad. He called me his left-hand man because I was left handed.

I would hide in the bathroom and light fires in the sink. There was something about fires that fascinated me. I was cruel to frogs by catching them, and leaving them in a box in the hot sun, then dumping them out.

I would hide under the table while watching TV with the family and suck my thumb. This was the only thing that soothed me. This became a focus of my mom. I would be ridiculed and humiliated by her. One night at the dinner table I picked up my napkin to find a wax thumb under the napkin. Everyone laughed at me. I was devastated. I made a decision to stop sucking my thumb at the age of 7.

I had bladder issues. I was detached from my body's feelings and very often wet my pants. At the age of six my mom threatened me that she was going to put diapers back on me if I didn't stop wetting my pants. She did this while a table full of her friends were there, I was so embarrassed.

I was living in "fight or flight" with no thought process. I desperately wanted someone to like me and tell me I was ok. There was no hope, no escape. I accepted that this was my life.

In grade seven I was reading at a grade two level. I would sit at the kitchen table trying to understand math problems but could not even read them, let alone understand them. My mom would say constantly, "Why do you refuse to learn?" She told me I was going to clean toilets for the rest of my life if I didn't learn. I didn't know how to learn; I was living in a state of constant fear, feeling flawed and lost.

Not only did my dad abuse me, he also abused my mother.

They would have raging fights. He would throw chairs, appliances, whatever he could find to threaten my mom. My sisters and I became very good at gauging when a fight was bubbling and we would flee – never knowing if our mom was going to be ok, or what we would have to do to clean up.

No one talked about the rage.

No one talked about anything.

To survive, I learned how to read my dad very well. Like I could read his mind. When I was working in his workshop with him, I taught myself to be able to know exactly what he needed next. This gave me some value in my mind and made me feel special.

TWO

Scab

———————

THERE WAS no hope of love or acceptance at home, that was a given in my life. I would go to school with a sliver of hope that I would be accepted there.

It didn't take long for the bullying and abuse from home to spill over to my peers. The two most popular kids in my grade were the leaders in my abuse at school. They started the ridicule and humiliation I endured. (To this day I still remember their names.) My grade two teacher encouraged the bullying. She wore tight sweaters, short skirts and go-go boots. She would stand up in front of the class and bring me up there to humiliate me about my thumb sucking. She gave the class permission to discipline me if they saw me sucking my thumb. When she handed out our papers she would tell everyone what each of us received on our papers. "D – again" as she put my paper on my desk.

I had eczema on my hands, arms and legs. My mom would put on this green cream and use old sheets to bandage the eczema. Because of this, the kids in my class decided to call me "Scab." They would say things like, "Don't touch that, Scab just touched it." I learned that I was ugly and homely.

A few days before Valentine's Day, in grade two, we made folders for the valentines we would receive from the kids. We decorated them, and the teacher taped them to our desks. I had no creativity or imagination. I would watch the other kids create and decorate. I tried to copy them and they would tell on me.

We were instructed by the teacher to come in a little earlier and place the Valentine's Day cards in the folders of our friends. I felt excited for the party. While I walked over to my desk, I noticed that everyone's folders were overflowing with valentines. I looked at my folder with excitement, but there were only three valentines in mine. My heart sank, I was devastated. The kids were all smirking and laughing at me.

In that moment, I came to believe I was unlovable. I shut down and stopped trying to learn.

This abuse at school went on from year to year. Always in the same class with the same kids. The boys would take advantage of my desperation and neediness by promising me friendship if I brought them things from home. I would bring Kool-Aid packages with sugar, or whatever they wanted, only to be laughed at and ridiculed by them saying, "You really believed that I would be friends with you?"

I stole school supplies from the teacher's desk. I would go to the bathroom and not return to class, just for some peace. One time I was caught with sticky tack for hanging up pictures that I had stolen, and the principal asked me where I got it from. I quickly lied and told her that my dad worked for the company.

I did have one friend: her name was Sarah-Jane. I was allowed to have sleepovers at Sarah-Jane's house. Subconsciously I was relieved when I was allowed to stay because I knew it was a safe place for me. I wasn't nice to Sarah-Jane or her mom. I stole and lied and got Sarah-Jane in trouble. Mrs. C, Sarah-Jane's mom, was amazing in spite of it all. After school she would have tea and cookies for us. She helped me write letters to my grandparents in England and she was special. When we entered the house, there was the smell of supper cooking. It was comforting to me. Mrs. C would take my sister and I on outings – Belmont theme park in Montreal, shopping and church.

This one time at church, I was in the classroom with all the kids. I was sitting on the floor listening to bible stories. There was this picture of Jesus, with a little girl sitting on his lap. There was this profound moment when I was flooded with this feeling of unconditional love. The sensation started at the tip of my head and rushed through my body. I spent my life trying to feel that again, not knowing what it was.

The school became concerned about my reading. My report cards had marks of D's (low grades but not quite failing), with the comment, "Sara is smart but she doesn't apply herself." I was put through a serious of tests to figure out what was wrong with me. My IQ came back quite high – however, I still wasn't learning.

I was labeled with "Dyslexia." My mom found a tutor for me, Mrs. J. Two days a week my mom would take me out of class to have tutoring downtown. That gave the kids another thing to make fun of, now I was also stupid. The tutoring didn't make any difference to me. I couldn't understand what she was teaching me.

The best part of the tutoring was one on one time with my mom. We would go to downtown Montreal to the farmer's market to buy meat and fresh eggs. I loved the fact that I was missing school. Mom would make me poached eggs on toast for lunch.

I don't know what age I was, I think seven or eight. I was looking in the mirror and realized that my eyes were the same colour as my father's.

At that moment, I made the decision that I must be evil.

I would wake up with panic attacks in the middle of the night. I would lie in bed, paralyzed with fear. I would think about what it would be like to die. I tried to imagine nothing because that was what I thought dying was like, entering a black hole of nothing. I thought to myself that I would never have children. Who would want to live in this horrible world?

In grade five, our teacher would read to the class. There was one book she read that was a collection of horror stories. At the end of one of the stories in the book, a man fell into an endless hole. The book confirmed a nameless terror..

The summer when I was about 8 or 9, I stayed at my aunt's – it was the longest two weeks of my life. She put me in the bedroom upstairs, farthest from hers. It was the bedroom my parents stayed in when we visited. There were two single beds in the room. She asked me if I was scared, then offered for one of my cousins to sleep in the extra bed. The first night my younger cousin stayed and he raped me. The second night my older cousin stayed and nothing happened. In later years I found out that he was gay. Being raped with no one to support me after, while out of my own environment, was even more devastating than being abused by my father.

At age nine or ten, I had this *bong, bong, bong* feeling in my head for several days. I didn't tell anyone because I was sort of numb to it. Lights were bothering me. Then a rash appeared on my arms and I showed my mom. She rushed me to the doctor. He told my mom to get me to the hospital. That was when I started to throw up. When I got there, they did a spinal tap and it was discovered I had Viral Meningitis. I stayed in the hospital for weeks. I felt safe in the hospital. When my dad came to visit me, I didn't want him there. For some reason I could feel his dark presence in my room.

My sisters and I took over the responsibility of trying to make my mom happy. We would buy her flowers, chocolates, whatever we could to please her. I would ride my bike to the store with money and buy my mom lipstick. I would feel happy when she was happy.

People-pleasing became my existence. I started to do housework and cook for my mom. She always complained about what to make for dinner. I wanted to make her happy. In some way it gave me a sense of control and worth over one part of my life as well. I could feel my mom's mood and I would gauge if it was a good time to ask for money that I needed for things like field trips or school supplies. I carried a feeling of not being deserving of things, which made it very difficult for me to ask for the basic needs. My mom would always give me the money begrudgingly. I was always the last student to bring in the permission slips and money for school events.

I went to Girl Guide camp when I was around ten. I hadn't developed social skills of any kind. I felt so lost and bad at camp. I wanted to go home. I cried at night. I wet my bed every night and peed my pants on many of the days. I told the leaders that I fell into puddles.

The final night of camp we had a huge bonfire. The leaders were giving out trophies for good deeds done. Then one of the leaders called me up to the front. I was quite proud of myself, thinking, *What am I being awarded for?* I stood in front of everyone and received a trophy for the one who fell into the most puddles. I was laughed at and humiliated.

The only means of escape from my life were food and TV. We would sit at Sunday dinner and eat big meals and watch Disney. Dinners were the only time when my family seemed happy.

The movies Cinderella and Snow White taught me that a Prince Charming was going to come along and rescue me. I longed for the day.

We would play a lot of board games as a family. I really did not like them. It was always a time when I felt even more stupid because I wasn't able to understand the games. If I didn't play I was ridiculed and humiliated by my dad saying I was being childish or silly. I hated having to stuff down my feelings, stuff down ME!

THREE

What Is This Feeling?

I AM TAKING a break from writing about my childhood. I kept feeling this pain while writing the first few chapters of this book. I wasn't able to identify what the feeling was, I had no words to give it. It was deeply rooted in me. I kept thinking that it was the sadness of my childhood and it would go away. It didn't!

I handwrote the first few chapters of this book. It was a great way to slow down and get in touch with my true feelings. What I didn't realize was how much the handwriting was going to affect me. Now, I'm going to share what I discovered.

The feeling of heaviness was getting stronger as I wrote. There was this one particular morning I woke up from a very restless sleep with the heaviness and ache so strong in my heart. I said to myself, *Sara, you need to sit down and figure out what this heaviness is.* I went to my meditation spot on the couch and thought about what was going on with me.

As I was sitting there with a coffee I began to think about what I had been writing. I thought back to where this heavy feeling was in my childhood memories. I became very aware of the emotional environment that I felt as a child. At home, my dad was abusing, humiliating and bullying me; at school I was being abused, humiliated and bullied by my peers. I felt as though I was living under water, breathing through a straw. It was damp, cold and dark. I was always looking up at these people on the surface of the water. My peers would be laughing at me, splashing water into my straw and watching me choke. They were laughing with each other, playing and enjoying their friends – they were the special people, the chosen ones. I thought of home – that was supposed to be my safe place, but instead it was a place of rage, anger, misery, humiliation and fear.

I tried to tell my mom so many times what was going on, how horrible school was – without having the words to explain the pain. I was shut down inside, lost, not connected to anyone, starved for a crumb of attention. She would tell me to get on with it and dismiss me.

There I was, sitting on the couch feeling all this pain from my childhood. I started working through the process of healing the emotional damage by doing a technique that my psychologist, Jane, taught me many years ago. It then occurred to me that remembering this time in my life made me feel hopeless. That's what the feeling was, hopelessness. No matter what I did, no matter how hard I tried, I had no escape, no way out. Day after day, month after month, year after year, for my whole life.

It was hopelessness, absolutely giving up on everything, including myself. Accepting and believing on a deep level that this was my life – to never to be popular, to never have happiness, love, acceptance or nurturing. I didn't even know what those things were – nurturing? This hopelessness was presenting itself as depression. I had become so good at hiding it from everyone on the outside and accepting it on the inside. It was all I knew. Waking up so many days with this depression. Dreading getting up in the morning, but pushing the feeling down and forcing myself to get up anyway, stuffing the feelings down and going through the motions. Feeling the ache, the insecurity, and the lack of meaning in my life.

As I was working through this hopelessness, another feeling came up. I sat with this feeling for a while, then realized it was a belief that I must be worthless. No value. I felt that it had to be true – that worthlessness was the reason why I was being treated so badly by everyone in my life. I had always put everyone else before me. The only way I knew how to survive all those years of sexual abuse was to put my dad on a pedestal and see him as a good person. My dad was my lifeline, my source of importance and if he was taken away, what would happen to me? Surely, I would die. I lived in terrorized fear of losing my dad, believing that I must be bad or worthless for him to harm me, since he was perfect. I saw him as my God.

To think that all these years later, after years of healing and working through those feelings, I discovered while writing my book that I was still living in a depression. How many of us feel this way now? Thinking that our current situation is hopeless, not realizing that it could be related to something that happened to us in our childhood? Still believing in the deep-rooted feeling of not being able to escape our situation now? Not being able to identify why we felt that way?

We go through the motions with this dread and believe it is just about where we are now, regardless of the situation. No matter how successful I have been in the past few years, none of that mattered to me deep down. I haven't been able to understand my success on a deep level, to celebrate it, or to feel the joy of it. The depression and hopelessness kept me captive and unable to feel anything good. The success I am talking about isn't just money – it is quality of life.

Using Jane's technique, I released the energy and emotional block around the memory while I sat there on the couch. Wow, it was surreal. There was this sadness that overtook me thinking of how long I have carried this pain.

As part of my healing process that I have been working through over the last years, I've become aware that it is very important to notice what you are feeling first thing in the morning. What I have found is that my subconscious emotions show up in my dreams. It wasn't important to remember what I was seeing in the dreams, but what I was feeling, and the emotions in the dream.

If you can become aware of what you're feeling as soon as you wake up, it can help you figure out if there are any underlying feelings you are not currently aware of. Think about it – while you are sleeping you are not on the defence, stuffing your emotions away or using any other behaviour to block the feelings. Since the consciousness that controls these behaviours is sleeping, your subconscious can allow these feelings to surface. Becoming aware of what you feel during your dreams is very powerful healing tool. You may find the memory or event in your past that those emotions are attached to, helping you to release the emotional pain.

I share the process I use to release the emotions from the memory and rewrite the story later on in this book. This process is a way of dealing with past trauma, helping you identify and release emotions that are attached to wounds that are holding you back.

I also need to mention that not all depression comes from our childhood. It can be chemical and hormonal and it is important to seek professional help to help find the root causes.

FOUR

Smile and Pretend

BACK TO THE STORY.

I started my period close to my 12th birthday. Things changed at home, my dad stopped abusing me. I was able to come out of hiding because the threat was gone. But I was three years old emotionally, with no cognitive thinking – numb, naïve, trusting charmers and players, and still struggling with school.

I had completely blocked the abuse from my memory.

We had moved away from Montreal; in fact, we had moved several times, and I was attending a different school again. I kept thinking that it was a new beginning – new friends and perhaps a good life – however, nothing changed. I kept attracting the same behaviour, the same bullying. I was put in special classes with kids that had learning disabilities. I hated it. My sister was an honour student and I was the dummy.

We had sex education at school. A nurse came into the class, split up girls from boys and talked about pads and condoms. I was completely lost but pretended to understand. We had never discussed body parts at home. One day my mom handed me a book, said, "Boys are going start noticing you now," and walked away. There was a picture of a girl with a white headband on the front cover and more pictures inside.

I learned personal care, like shaving my legs, from friends. My mother never wanted to discuss anything like that with me.

My focus became boys and strong sexual feelings. My education about relationships was abuse, TV shows like *The Love Boat*, romantic songs and sexual feelings. I was longing for someone, anyone, to pay attention to me, with a gut-wrenching ache in my soul. This was a recipe for disaster. I was cute, able to hide my truth, with a core belief that I was bad, ugly, and not worth anything. I had the "Cinderella Syndrome" belief that a prince was going to come and rescue me.

I came home from school one day and noticed a couple black suitcases by the garage door. My dad sat the three of us on the couch. He and my mom stood front of us, and my mom was upset. I knew something serious was going on. My dad began to tell us that he did not love my mom anymore. That he was moving to the YMCA. I wasn't sure how I felt. On one level, I did not really like my dad, but on another, he was abandoning our family.

My mom was devastated. She cried all the time and cried on my shoulder. That tore at my heart.

A few weeks later my sister showed me a letter she had found that my mom had written. My dad was having an affair. That was why my mom was so devastated, after all those years of being devoted to him through thick and thin. Now, he was cheating on her.

I have no idea what happened but the next thing I knew my dad moved back in and nothing was talked about, except that we were moving again – this time to New Brunswick.

We lived in a very nice town in New Brunswick. The people were very friendly and great neighbours. I met my first real boyfriend at thirteen. We would go driving in his Chevy Impala. We did a lot of necking and petting and hanging out with friends, drinking beer. I would come home past my curfew and try to sneak into the house. Sometimes I would be drunk and my sister would try to sober me up with coffee.

We lasted eleven months in New Brunswick, my mom didn't like it much. She was used to big cities. It was off to Vancouver. I was devastated about leaving my boyfriend. I cried on the plane, I cried for months. We wrote letters for six months or so. Then I stopped writing, I found other boys to pay attention to.

FIVE

Get the F*** Out

WE ARRIVED in Vancouver and moved into a hotel for six weeks while my parents looked for a new house. It was summer and there was a pool. My sister had a bathing suit given to her and she offered the suit to me. I put it on and my dad walked into the room. He grabbed the top of the bikini and ripped it off me, accusing me of being a "slut." I had no idea what a "slut" was, but I was devastated.

A new school again, new friends, but I felt inferior to all of them. I had learned to be very charming and sexy. I lived in a lost place, in emotional pain, full of shame, guilt, worthlessness and resentment. My life felt like I was living in a play. No reality. I had no idea how to react or what to say when I was in situations or out socially, I felt awkward and flawed. I had no identity, no sense of self and no decision-making tools. I lived like a pinball bouncing from situation to situation. I had no real feelings for anything or anyone. Disconnected from myself. I needed either someone else to live through, or something to take away the pain.

Thank God, my mom had put the fear of drugs in us. Drugs were everywhere and I was terrified to try them. Alcohol was my drug of choice.

I would skip out of classes to hang out with the smokers. I had started smoking when I was eleven, sneaking cigarettes from my parents. I would bring them for the other kids as a way to get them to like me. I cheated on exams, I lied all the time to everyone. Lying was a way of life for me. It came so naturally.

At the end of grade nine we had a school dance and I met a guy who was one grade older than me. He was tall and I felt safe with him. He played basketball and was on the first string. That gave me a feeling of being special and a sense of belonging because I was with a popular guy.

We became a couple, hung out together and had sex. I would come home from being with him, feeling so ashamed of myself, dirty, just horrible. My mom did not like him. A few times I tried to break up with him, but the pain I felt was so gut-wrenching when he was not in my life, that we would get back together.

I began to hang out with the party kids. We would drink every weekend and that's how I was able to break up with the guy I was dating: the parties and alcohol became my way of escaping instead. There were always drugs available at the parties, but I never touched them. I was terrified what the drugs would do to me. I knew girls that were doing them and seemed out of control. Drugs scared me!

I managed to graduate. I have to say that I had some amazing teachers at Argyle, who reached out to me. Mr. George Saunders was a counsellor at the school, and somehow, he knew that there was something wrong with me. We would meet for coffee and talk. Mr. Saunders always said that if there was anything I needed to tell him, that he was in a safe place for me to share with him. I didn't understand what he meant. My dad was not happy with the relationship I had with Mr. Saunders and indicated that perhaps Mr. Saunders had ulterior motives. I felt so confused because my dad didn't say much about my life, in fact he was not involved in my life at all anymore. So, when he said something it had an impact on me.

It was later in my life when I realized that Mr. Saunders knew my story. I called him when I was in my thirties and asked him, "How did you know?" Mr. Saunders said he could tell by my body language and my insecurities. I told him I was trying to understand my past. I talked with him for a while, then he told me an interesting thing: the school division was just trying to decide if the counselling program really helped, and whether they were going to cut it from the school. I don't know what was decided in the end, but he was very happy to hear from me.

My grade twelve English teacher was amazing. I was still reading and writing at a very low-grade level. My mom helped me write an essay for the final exam. I was to take it into class and use it to write the essay. I lost the paper. I frantically looked for it but could not find it. I was devastated. I went to class and wrote my teacher a letter explaining what had happened. She graded my letter and passed me.

I graduated, which gave me some self-confidence that perhaps I could be successful at something.

My dad was still raging and cutting my mom down as he always had, but with this new sense of confidence I had, it started to bother me. I was really hating him. In fact, I wasn't liking anyone in my family at that point. The family would all sit and talk about things that did not matter. Surface conversations. I felt like an outsider looking in. I was a cool kid and they were nerds. The rebellious side was coming out. I was seventeen and finally free from school and the need of my parents in my life.

During that summer, I did what I wanted, when where I wanted. I often slept at a girlfriend's just to not be home. When I was home I hid in my room. I would read the newspaper for places to rent. Trying to figure out how I was going to afford $75 a month rent. I didn't want to be there, yet I had no idea how I was going to get away.

I had no plans for the future, never thought about university. My school studies were not focused on any direction. I did love to cook.

One afternoon I walked into the kitchen. There was my 6'2" dad leaning over my mom while she was sitting in a chair. Once again, he was telling her that she was too stupid to go back to school, in his bullying rage. That was enough! I snapped and yelled, "I don't like you treating my mom that way."

Next thing I knew he had grabbed my arm and pushed me upstairs to my bedroom. He threw open my window and out went my bedding. My blanket, sheets, pillow on the grass. Then he turned to me and said, "If you don't like what goes in this house, then get the fuck out!"

That was all I needed. The next week I found a place to stay with two party girls just off of Lonsdale, close to all the action. We would go to the local bars, get drunk and dance. We were all under age.

I found a job working for a jean store – sales to which I was quite good – making $3.50 an hour. The owner of the store was very hard on me. She accused me of hustling clients and her husband. She gave me jobs like cleaning the tar off the floor. I did what I was told trying to please her. Regardless, I was fired. I didn't understand.

Then I was hired by a bank. The girls had constant parties until 2 a.m., keeping me awake at all hours. I would fall asleep at my desk, and was fired from that job.

I found another job and I moved into a condo by myself. I did not like being on my own. The emotional pain I was living in was intolerable, and I began having sex with whoever paid attention to me. I would wake up with men I didn't know.

I began to realize that something was not right. Mr. Saunders had sparked something in me – to start searching for answers. The only challenge was, I didn't yet know what the questions were. Mr. Saunders had given me the book *"Your Erroneous Zones"* by Wayne Dyer. One evening I was sitting on a bus trying to muster my way through this book. Not really understanding much except for these words, "You can choose what you want in your life." I looked at my reflection in the bus window and thought, *I can choose?*

This was when I made a decision to stop lying to people. I began to lie in my early years to cover up what was happening to me. Even when I told the truth no one believed me. My life was so shallow I told lies to give my life some meaning. I didn't want to do that any more. Although I was living in a lie to myself under the surface, I still tried to be truthful to people in my life. If I lied, I would catch myself and correct the story to the truth as I knew it.

SIX

No Sense of Self

I HAD no respect for myself, no self care. When I was eighteen I found myself pregnant, not sure who the father was. I went to the doctor who told me I could have an abortion. I was relieved. I had the abortion without much thought or care. My sister helped me, picked me up from the hospital. The next night I was out partying and clubbing again.

I started to bleed heavier and heavier until the toilet was full of blood. I told my friend and she said it was normal. She was only interested in partying. I was hemorrhaging. I went home that night and crawled into bed. When I woke up two days later, I crawled out of bed, feeling so weak. I went back to work at the clothing store and life carried on. I never went to the doctor.

I was trying to figure things out. I felt so frustrated and confused most of the time. I didn't have the ability to see forward, dream or see a future for me. I took a program at the college to learn skills to work in an office. There had to be something I could do for work. I felt so lost.

It was very challenging to find a job I liked, I became very bored quickly and I didn't want people to know I was a fake. I heard from someone that Safeway paid great money and great benefits. So, I contacted Safeway one day while I was working at a reception job. I managed to get through to the HR department. As I was chatting with the HR guy, another phone line lit up. I told him that I would call him back. He said just put me on hold. I refused to put him on hold and said that I didn't like putting people on hold. I hung up and called him back. He was very impressed with the fact I did not put him on hold and invited me for an interview.

Safeway hired me. I did my job well. I was a people pleaser, worked above and beyond. I loved the fast checkout because it kept me busy. I had regulars and made great money. I was also becoming aware of my moods. Some days worked so well and others I was in a bad place emotionally. I was so insecure and was terrified to sit with the other cashiers. If another cashier asked me to go for lunch with them, I made an excuse. I could not sit one on one with other people. I thought I was stupid and didn't have anything to talk about.

There were a lot of parties and drugs with the staff at this job. I would go to the parties and I was asked to do cocaine, I said no thanks and watched them. They were very respectful of that.

We made great money – I was renting with my sister and we paid $172 a month for rent between the two of us. But I never had enough to get through the week: shopped constantly, spent money on whatever I wanted to make me feel better. I didn't know how to budget, plan or set goals. Lived for what ever would take the pain away.

My sister invited me to a wedding of two of her friends. When I was there I met a friend of hers. He was a good guy. We danced all night, and began to date. We would laugh and have so much fun together. He would drive all night from Smithers to see me every other weekend. When he left I would cry.

After eight months of dating I met one of his best friends at The Bay. We were chatting for a while and Mac said that his buddy had found the girl he was going to marry. I remember thinking, *I wonder who that is?* It was a few days later when I realized it was me. I had never even thought about marriage. Nor that he felt that way.

Shortly after that, my dad showed up at my work. I was working at the till, looked behind me and there he was, standing there staring at me. I was so surprised to see him there, he had never been at my work before. I asked for a break and walked out side the store with him. He had a granola bar in his pocket and offered it to me. We walked down the street and I felt like a little girl again. 3 years old. He bought me a coffee and sat down on the bench. My dad proceeded to tell me that I should not be dating my sister's friends. It was not fair to her and he couldn't believe I was doing that to her. I was ridden with guilt and shame.

My dad still had control over my life. His goal was to keep me isolated and alone to keep the family secret. He had controlled me through guilt and shame in my teens and was now doing it again.

I did what I was told. Stuffed my feelings and broke up with him. I believe that was the evening he was going to ask me to marry him. He was heartbroken, I was numb. A few months later he contacted me and asked me if I was sure. I assured him I was.

What I found out years later was he had asked my dad for my hand in marriage. My dad gave him his blessing, but then guilted me into breaking up with him. He was a great guy and I loved him the best I knew how to love anyone.

After that, my choices in men began to spiral downhill fast. I began to date a pot smoker. I tried drugs for the first time with him and his buddies. They were also into hash oil. We all smoked a joint then went down to White Spot. There I sat while stoned, with people I did not know. I became paranoid. I had to endure sitting there and talking myself out of freaking out in my head. That was enough for me, I made a decision not to touch drugs again.

I became pregnant a few months into the relationship and we decided to marry.

I had a miscarriage.

I thought getting married was what was going to make me feel better.

We were divorced a year and seven months later.

SEVEN

No More!

I MET DON AT SAFEWAY. When I was working he came through my till several times. He had two children, a little girl and an older boy. Don asked me out. He was good looking, blond, charming, and he needed help with the kids. He invited me for dinner and after dinner massaged my feet. I slept over that night.

I had noticed some items at the house that belonged to a woman and a few days later, when I was coming in the house, she was there. She looked at me in a scary way, and told me that he was not a nice guy. I thought she was jealous.

Don was employed with the movie industry. Worked long hours and left me with the kids. He never asked me to take care of the kids, it was assumed. I had to find people to take care of them when I was working.

These kids were out of control. I had no self-worth or esteem or identity and the kids walked all over me. They were back and forth from Don's home to their mother's home in Ontario. For two years, I tried to deal with the kids acting out. The boy peed on stuffed animals and the girl had raging fits. I thought there was something wrong with me as a caregiver.

We bought a four-bedroom house together. It was a nice home. I quit my job at Safeway to care for the kids and the household. I had a $1200 a month allowance just for me. I really thought my life was getting better. Although it was complete chaos, at least I was needed. By the time we moved into the house, Don had complete emotional control over me. He had slowly taken control over me by raging, cutting me down, and corrected everything I was doing; building on my insecurities and pain I was in. I didn't do anything with out his approval.

I was living in fear.

Shortly after we moved in, I found out that I was pregnant. Don was not pleased and suggested an abortion. I knew I was meant to have the baby and I wanted it. He had his kids, why couldn't I? The kids went back to live with their mom at this time. He started to drink more and became more and more abusive to me.

One evening after Don had been drinking large amounts of scotch, he became physically abusive. He had me pinned up against the kitchen cabinets and a lioness came out of me. I raised my hand and hit him in the face. My fingernail poked his eye and he let me go. He turned around and backhanded me in the head.

He ended up with a black eye. He told everyone at work that a rock flew out of the lawnmower and hit him in the eye. He told me that the make-up crew were taking pictures of his eye as it was a perfect black eye. I learned to stay away from him.

The pregnancy was long and I didn't like how I felt. There was no support from Don. The kids were back living with us towards the end of my pregnancy. Their mother had been charged with fraud again and was unable to care for them. They were wild children. Don left them in my care for seventeen-hour days. He would come home drunk, or high on cocaine, oblivious and without regard to the fact that I close to term.

My due date was December 24th which came and went. I had not done any prenatal classes. Had no idea what I was doing.

New Year's Eve we celebrated with a glass of champagne, that's when my labour began. By 5 a.m. my contractions were five minutes apart. I contacted my doctor and he informed me he was up at

Whistler and was unable to be there. That upset me. I called my sister to come stay with the kids, I woke up Don to drive me to the Richmond General. As we were driving he took great care to hit every bump he could. I was so uncomfortable.

At noon, the contractions were still five minutes apart. Don was getting agitated and wanted to leave to buy cigarettes. The on-call doctor was concerned because I had developed shingles on the inside of my leg with all the stress I was living in. He consulted another doctor and they concurred that the baby should not be in contact with shingles. It could cause blindness. I was told that I was going to have a C-section and was prepared for surgery. Don couldn't wait to get out of there and left.

I was using laughing gas to deal with the labour pains, and I was relieved that I was having a C-section and relaxed. The hospital staff took me down to the OR and left me in this room outside of the OR. Alone. The room was cold and dark. The labour pains became more and more intense. I had no gas and no one to support me. I hung on to the bed railing for dear life, trying to deal with the contractions. I was holding my breath, trying to handle the excruciating pain. It was awful.

I could hear the nurses and doctors chatting in the background, laughing and kidding around with each other about their New Year's parties. There I was in complete desperation, hanging on for dear life. Dismissed. Ignored.

I had no idea how long I was in this state of despair when a nurse came up to me and realized what was going on – that my labour had advanced quickly. She rushed me into the OR. I was transferred onto the operating table and prepared for surgery.

They pinned my arms down, put an IV in my hand, and hooked up monitors to the baby's heart and my heart. There was this nurse trying to paint iodine on my belly. I kept wanting to put my knees up but she kept pushing them down aggressively, telling me to "STOP." The smell was horrid. There were two heartbeats in the distance and all these people I did not know. I had no trust in anyone.

Then an oxygen mask was placed on my face. It was stuffy and

29

smothering, but I couldn't get my hands free to remove it. The contractions were so painful and I had no control. I felt discarded, like nobody in that room gave a shit about me – no one had even bothered to talk to me. Who were these people? THE PAIN!!... and then panic took me to another place.

A doctor walked towards me and tried to console me by telling me that I was probably going to have the New Year's baby for Tsawwassen... It was too late, I was in terrifying panic. I could feel my eyes bulging like a wild animal in distress. I was trying to free myself. Terror took me! My body began to stiffen up. The nurse on my left looked behind me to the doctor and said, "Excuse me Doctor, can't you tell your patient is panicking?"

What?

I lost it.

All the abuse I had endured my whole life: the men, my father, all the ways I had abused myself. The pain, the self-loathing, the hope-lessness. Living in debilitating fear. Constant stress, stuffing every-thing down inside of me, believing that somehow, I deserved all of it. Now my physical body was in massive pain as well. The contractions, the nurse not letting me put my legs up, being pinned down, and the doctor not even being aware of the state I was in.

In that moment, I decided: that was it, NO MORE!!! I was done, I was not doing this any more... In my complete desperation, I cried out in my mind, *GOD, I WANT TO DIE.* I meant it from the depth of my soul.

EIGHT

Home

WITH THOSE WORDS, *I want to die*, I left the room, the physical pain, the panic. I fell back into the bed. Then I looked up. There was a dark space, black and calling me. As I headed towards the darkness, I could feel this horrific emotional pain, a deep ache, with moaning, screaming and fear. The horror became stronger and stronger. I could hear voices calling me: "Sara, come." I could see painful faces. The ache in my soul was so deep.

Not too sure how long I was there heading towards that darkness. It felt like a lifetime.

All of a sudden, I thought these words, *PLEASE FORGIVE ME*. I wasn't sure who I was asking forgiveness from, but I meant it whole-heartedly. Instantly I turned to my right, away from the horror and to a light – a lovely soft light of absolute peace. The peace was beyond words. This peace filled me. The most incredible part of this place was the unconditional acceptance of who I was, right then and there in all my mess. Love filled my soul. My spirit was being renewed. The beautiful pink light filled me with comfort, a comfort I had not had for a long time. As I floated up I kept saying, *"I know that... Oh, I know that..."* I knew this place. The experience and conversation continued, in a way that is difficult to put into words...

I was home.

Floating to the crest of the light, I was being filled with such love, such grace, wholeness and a sense of renewal. Lovely beyond Lovely. When I arrived at the crest of the light I stopped. There was this lovely presence asking me, "Are you sure this is what you want?"

I knew by then that it was not time, so I said, *"No, I need to go back and do what I was meant to do."*

Instantly, I felt myself and everything around me begin to spin. The light was spinning with the darkness around me and with me. It spun faster and faster, then entered my body through the top of my head. It was like a tornado funnel entering me. Then there I was – I looked up and saw ripples, like rain drops on a puddle in front of my eyes. There was a humming noise in my ears, and I realized, '*Oh, I am under anesthetic.*" Then I settled back into my body.

I woke up in the recovery room. The nurse congratulated me on a new baby girl. She was a big one, 9 lb 10 oz. I fell asleep again.

I didn't wake up again until 7 p.m. that night. I was overtaken by disappointment that here I was back in this body, with the pain. I had bitten the inside of my mouth, every muscle in my body was hurting and I had a hemorrhoid the size of an egg. I was sad that I was back but realized this was where I was meant to be. I buzzed the nurse to bring me my baby.

I unraveled the blanket and looked at her. She was beautiful.

That evening Don came to visit me. I was very tired, he left very quickly. He wanted to look at my belly and made a nasty comment about it looking like a prune. I thought, *"I don't like you."* Not sure if he even saw the baby.

When I woke up the next morning, the peace was still with me. The nurse that had first come over to me in the OR waiting room came to see me, asking if I was ok. I looked at her and said, "I know I died."

She never said a word.

NINE

The Profound Change

I WAS NOT THE SAME.

I could feel people's energies. A nurse came in to see how breast-feeding was going. She was mean and aggressive in trying to tell me what to do. I could feel it, didn't like what I was feeling and I told her to leave my room.

After my baby was asleep, I sat on my bed looking out the window at Richmond Park. Off in the distance, a family was skating on the pond. A mom, a dad and a little girl. I watched how they interacted, floating around, playing with the little girl. It was beautiful. I thought to myself, *"That's what I want for my baby."*

I was in the hospital for a week. I was sharing with the nurses that I wasn't really wanting to go back home. Don had only come to see me twice in the week. I didn't like his energy. It was very dark, even though he put on a charming face. But what else was I going to do? I had a new baby, no job, no other place to live.

I went back to the house, focusing on my baby, Kathleen. She was such a good baby. Four hours between feedings, healthy and beautiful. Don was working again; the two kids were with living with us. I was coping. Then Don brought home a new puppy.

I had just had surgery, and now I was looking after a new baby, two kids and a new puppy all on my own. The puppy was throwing up, Kathleen needed my full attention and the kids were out of control.

After a few days, I took the puppy back to the pet store. Don was not pleased with my new-found confidence.

A month or so after Kathleen's birth, I was changing her on the change table. Don's little girl came into the bedroom and climbed up on the stool. Out of the blue I said to her, "If anyone ever touched you here, would you tell me?" She looked down and slipped out of the room without a word. I knew the way she left that something was wrong.

I contacted Social Services and took the kids to their office. The kids were interviewed and so was I. Don was contacted and inter- viewed. He came back to the house where I was. I requested to have a social worker at the house because I was very fearful of what Don would do. I felt so bad, I was so confused. The next day the kids were sent back home to live with their mother. I went to my sister's and stayed there.

I was in shock, confused and terribly scared. Time seemed to slip by. The family got involved and my parents cancelled a trip to Hawaii. When my mom was visiting my sister and I, my dad called. He wanted to talk to me and he was furious at me, saying, "Typical of you to cause trouble when we were planning to go away." He was trying to lay guilt and shame on me. In the conversation he said to me, "I know nothing about sexual abuse."

I couldn't figure out why he was reacting towards me like that. Laying guilt on me in my time of need. There was no support from him at all. I didn't even know they were planning to go away. I remember thinking that the conversation was very weird.

I didn't want to stay with my sister either. I felt confused there too. I ended up in a woman's shelter with Kathleen. It was horrible – she cried all the time, and I was struggling emotionally to understand what the heck was going on. I called Don and he convinced me to come home. I ended up going back to the house.

Things settled the best they could. I focused on raising Kathleen. I kept trying to find answers to what had happened to me. Went to a few churches to talk to pastors. One pastor said I was "in the arms of Abraham" during the near-death experience. I went to the doctor that was in the OR and told him that if anyone else dies at his table, he was to tell them. The changes were so profound.

One evening I was in Kathleen's room, sitting in the rocking chair feeding her. Classical music was playing very softly in the background. It was a very tender moment between her and I. Don arrived home and came to the bedroom door. There was this pink glow in the room. He stood back with his eyes wide open and said, "WOW." He could not enter the room.

I kept trying to convince Social Services that I had made a mistake about Don. The kids were put into counselling in Ontario, against the wishes of both Don and their mother. I thought it was so odd that the parents didn't care. The kids ended up at a program called "Crèche," counselling for ritual and sexual abuse. I was told by a counsellor that they had never seen kids so damaged from ritual abuse before. She asked me if there were things in the house like books with a dictionary with meanings for symbols or an ox skull. I thought, *What?* I couldn't understand what she was talking about.

That started me questioning what was going on.

I was trying to understand why my life wasn't working any more. I kept trying to fit back in with my old ways, but I wasn't able to tolerate the people in my life, I was seeing things so differently. I wrote my parents a letter telling them I didn't like way they treated me. I thought if I said something, things would change. They never discussed the letter with me and completely ignored the fact I wrote it.

When Kathleen was just over a year and we were visiting my parents for my dad's birthday, and I noticed my dad trying to build trust with her. He took her over to the floor to ceiling window where she was frightened of, then he comforted her and held her hand. And said words to her. I could see he was building her sense of trust in him. That bothered me and I wasn't sure why. I didn't want him near her.

Valentine's Day night I received a call from my sister. It was late, she said, "Dad died."

"What?"

"Dad had a massive heart attack and died."

That night I felt his presence at the foot of my bed and he said, "Goodbye." Two weeks before his death I had a dream he had died and now it was true!

There were over 400 people at his funeral. I had such mixed feelings. On one level it was like a root was pulled up in my life and on another, relief that he was gone. I felt so confused and guilty.

After he died I began searching for answers about my life. I started watching self-help shows like the PBS feature on John Bradshaw's book *"The Family."* The series that John had on PBS made so much sense to me. The dysfunctional family – the rebel, me. My older sister, the responsible one; and my younger, the jokester. I bought the book and read it. I couldn't figure out what the addiction was in my family. My dad drank but was not a drunk – but we were definitely a dysfunctional family.

I found Melody Beattie's books. Read them, started her daily affirmations. I began to watch the Oprah show and became obsessed with her guests.

When Kathleen became two, Don told me I had done a good job with her. I remember thinking that it was a very odd comment. Then Kathleen started to act differently. She was acting out things like, "Here is your puppy, here is mine."

Where was that coming from, I wondered? I was her only caregiver and Don worked seventeen-hour days.

One morning I went to check on Kathleen when she had slept in, which was unusual for her. She wasn't her usual self. Her energy was dark. I took her downstairs and sat her on the counter. Don was in my eyesight and I said, "Something is wrong with Kathleen." I watched him look concerned, then he told me that I was being ridiculous. I knew.

I left that night, packed up what I could. I was terrified, yet clear. My world was so messed up. Yet I had a strong sense of spirit. I could no longer live the way I was, but how was I supposed to live?

I went into hiding. Don would hunt me down and harass me. I then moved into my mom's home with an alarm system. He would phone my mom's house a hundred times a day. I began to realize how much mind-controlled and mentally abused I was, because he still had a pull on me. For the first few months I was like a "deer in the headlights." I was watching a TV show one day and I heard these words: "Information is power, so don't give him any." I stopped talking to him. As time went on with no contact with Don, I began to clear my thinking.

Six months later, my mom and I got into a huge argument. I packed up Kathleen and moved.

Before the near-death I was living in the play, doing what I was told, stuffing my true feelings down. Now, it was like I was living in the audience, sitting and watching a play. The play was about how I had created my life before being reconnected to my spirit. I could see all this stuff in front of me. These issues with people in my life, how they treated me. Every time I tried to go back into the play, it no longer worked.

I had no answers, and I couldn't figure out what the questions were either. I often found myself overtaken with fear, anxiety and depression. I had days when I couldn't get out of bed. Kathleen would lie there with me. I was terrified that Don would find us, I would have nightmares. This was a very tough time for me, holding on by a thread.

One night I was watching TV and Tony Robbins was speaking to an audience. He said something like, if you only make a 5% change in your life today, that the change would grow bigger. In that moment, I made a decision to do what I could to deal with this state I was in.

I began searching and started to attend a church. There was some comfort there. I was hoping someone would help me understand what had happened to me on the operating table and why my life was in such a mess. In those days there were no computers, no google, just TV, books and people.

I met Marlene at church and she invited me to a bible study at her house. I was very insecure with the ladies and I felt very uncomfortable there. She shared the gospel with me, the part about asking Jesus in to my life. It didn't make sense to me. I was at the crest of the light already without asking Jesus into my life. Or had I asked Jesus into my life years before when I was at church with Mrs. C, and I was overtaken by unconditional love?

Marlene gave me an old bible of hers. I graciously accepted it. She had underlined many passages throughout the book with a red pen.

Social Services offered me counselling and I felt I needed support. Going through this counselling, I discovered that Kathleen had been through some ritual abuse. My heart sank, the counsellor at the Creche program was right. She had asked me if there were thing around the house at would identify cult activity. I didn't understand what she was asking or suggesting - it was to far fetched for me to comprehend.

Now my daughter was showing signs of ritual abuse. I was told that Don was a member of a satanic cult. How the hell did I end up with a man that was with a cult?

That's when fear took over me. My past was not me anymore. What was my life supposed to be? I had no reference point to feed from, no history. I came to this point of standing at the balcony's sliding door. The outside was too big and the condo was too small. I was freaking out. I looked at this stool in the corner of the room. The bible Marlene had given me was on the stool. I grabbed the bible and opened it up. There on the page I opened, underlined in red, were these words: "Do not fear them, for the Lord your God is the one fighting for you" (Deuteronomy 3:22). In that moment, I realized I had to put complete trust in God, focus on him and not the fear. I kept repeating the passage in my head.

Then and there I started praying and asking God to take the fear from me. I found comfort in those words, knowing that there was someone looking out for me. It was important to have faith and trust. This was my lifeline. The trust started with a thread – every time I found myself in fear, which was most of the time, I reminded myself to think of God and the fear would stop. It was important that I took the focus off Don and onto the loving myself and my healing.

TEN

Reality Check

_____

AS I AM WRITING these chapters, I am thinking to myself, *"How did I cope with this?"*

I met a woman my age at the bible study I was attending. She was in the process of leaving her husband and we decided to share a house. She had two girls close to Kathleen's age and I thought it would be good for both of us. A short time later, I learned her new boyfriend was into spirit guides. He claimed to channel *"White Feather"*. He wanted to introduce the spirit guides to me. I refused.

After moving in with her, I attended a golf awards dinner with a friend. There was this tall guy sitting at a table. I kept looking at him and his friend noticed. He came over and we started chatting. Later that evening he walked me to my car and kissed me. He seemed like a decent guy, went to church, loved his mom. He had a niece that he had a good relationship with and I thought he would be a great influence on Kathleen. Things had begun to get a little crazy where I was living; my roommate started accusing me of eating her food and using her makeup. She told me that my daughter was making her very angry and threatened to hurt her. I shared this with my new guy, he had a suite in the basement of his house and invited us to stay there.

We moved in.

Within a few months, we became involved, it seemed like a good situation for everyone. I took over household duties, cooked for him and raised Kathleen. He provided financially and we settled into being a little family. It was nice to feel like we belonged. I felt safe for the first time in a long time.

Don had started court proceedings to have visitations with Kathleen. He hadn't seen her for over two years as I had I refused to let that happen. A Long Section 15 had been ordered by the judge – meaning that a counselor would interview both parties and come up with recommendations for the child. I met with the counsellor. He could see my fears and asked me give him a reason to back up my fears. In that moment, I remembered the words the counselor at the "Crèche" program had said about how damaged Don's kids were. I asked the counselor to call them in Ontario. I received a call a few days later by the counselor telling me that he had never done this before but was recommending the father have no visitation rights. I was so relieved. That was behind me. Then the support payments stopped. I made a decision to let them go. It was important that I didn't have contact with him. We had a new life.

I was awarded sole custody of Kathleen.

A few months later, I was pregnant with a sister for Kathleen. My new man and I married.

I didn't talk much anymore about my near-death experience. I seemed to be in a better place. I was raising Kathleen, my life was seeming more balanced, and I didn't want people to think I was crazy.

One evening I was watching the show *Nova*. I don't remember which particular episode, but it was about people who had experienced a Near-Death. These people were sharing their stories with terminal cancer patients. This program was a way of giving cancer patients insight as to what to expect about dying. I couldn't believe it. *OH MY GOD*, they were talking about me. They each shared their experience and how it had completely changed their life. I quickly grabbed a VCR tape and popped it in and pushed record. I sat there watching this show in awe. The doctor/researcher was explaining how profound the changes were in these people's lives. That the NDE

(Near-Death Experience) gave them a strong sense of connection to something else beyond life, and they lost their fear of dying. They were no longer caught up in the things of the world but felt a greater purpose for their lives.

I wasn't crazy!

That show gave me such peace, knowing that there were other people out there that had experienced dying. (There wasn't internet then, things were not shared like they are now.) To know that I wasn't crazy was such a relief. I kept watching the video over and over, each time feeling more relieved by hearing about others' Near-Death Experiences.

During the pregnancy, I developed Crohn's. I was very ill. It became apparent that my new husband found golf to be more important than me. At one point, I was completely dehydrated and very sick. Every time I tried to eat I wanted to throw up. I kept telling him I needed to go to the hospital, but he didn't want to take me. I accepted this behaviour from him because I was terrified of being alone with both physical and emotional pain.

One morning, I insisted he take me to the hospital. As soon as we went through the door when we arrived, the nurse immediately rushed me into emergency, put me in a bed and put an IV in me. I was a skeleton with a big baby belly. I knew I was sick, but I had been in denial about how bad it had gotten.

They did a stress test for the baby, she was ok. I was hospitalized for seven days while my symptoms settled down.

When I was leaving the hospital, the attending physician told me that he wanted me on Prednisone – I said, "No way!" Prednisone was well known in my family – eczema, asthma, and illnesses – so I knew the side effects.

Then he said, "What do you think we have been putting in your IV?" I was thirty weeks pregnant. How was that going to affect the baby? I was mad. He then proceeded to tell me not to try natural alternatives, they did not work. I thought at that moment, *I am going to look into alternatives.* That reinforced my disbelief in the medical establishment.

I refused to go through labour because of the experience I had during the birth of Kathleen. I was terrified of panicking again. The doctor was very understanding and scheduled a C-section to have the baby. The birthing experience was peaceful for me. Her father was there to hold her as soon as she was born.

I gave birth to a beautiful baby girl. She was long and lean. It became apparent shortly after birth that she had health issues. She was screaming a lot, sleeping for only forty-five minutes at a time. She had an eye infection which led to putting her penicillin for her first few weeks of life. Her father wanted me to let her scream. I knew she was in some sort of discomfort and I couldn't let her scream. I couldn't believe his cold heart.

Eight weeks after giving birth, my husband and I were being intimate. In an instant, I had a flash of my childhood. There I was on top of my father, having sex. I immediately changed the position we were in and tried to block it.

The next morning, I knew. I knew that my dad had sexually abused me. It was like the veil was lifted. Oh my God, that was what it was! I remembered watching an *Oprah Show* on sexual abuse. Oprah asked the guest, "Isn't it true that if you think you have been sexually abused, you probably have?" That comment resonated with me. I kept questioning if I had or not.

The flashback put me into emotional turmoil. On one level, I was relieved that I finally figured it out, but on another, I was devastated. I kept thinking *Oh my God.* Then the next thing I began to think about was my mother. I knew she would freak with this news. I didn't talk to her for weeks.

The phone rang one morning. We didn't have call display then, I answered it without thinking and there was my mom on the other end. She kept asking me what was wrong, I refused to tell her. Then she said, "What is it, sexual abuse?"

I said, "Yes. Dad sexually abused me." Our relationship changed completely that day.

My mom told my grandparents what I was saying about my dad. Even though they were my mom's parents they idolized him. My grandparents disowned me, refused to ever see me again. I saw my grandmother once again in the next five years on her 100th birthday. I saw my grandpa once before he died at 97.

Punished for something I never asked for, something that was done to me by my father. That hurt me so deeply, I felt abandoned and terribly alone. That was when I started to realize how enmeshed my life was with my family's. I had carried so much responsibility for my mother's happiness that I had pushed the secret into hiding. My mom and I began fighting all the time.

I saw my mom a few more times after telling her about what he had done to me. She so desperately wanted me to retract what I had said about her husband. In some ways, I wanted to retract it too. I hated knowing the truth but I knew I was right. I had a bigger responsibility to heal myself – for me and for my girls.

Within the year, my husband lost his job and we decided to move to the Okanagan. In some way, I thought I could run from the issues that I was facing. I did maintain my girls' relationships with my mom and grandparents. I would bring them for visits and my sister would take them to see the family.

It was a very sad, hurtful time for me.

ELEVEN

Healing Crohn's and Colitis

I STARTED to ask for guidance for things I needed to get help with in my life. If I had something that I wanted to understand, I would ask the universe for understanding. It was quite simple: *Show me what this feeling is; Show me what to do about this; Show me how to heal Crohn's.*

My prayers would be answered with something I heard: on the TV, in a book, or what someone would say to me. If I heard it twice then I knew it meant something to me – that it was the answer. The trick was to be open to the answers because I never knew where they would be coming from.

I asked the universe to show me how to heal my Crohn's and help my daughter.

One afternoon I was driving past the mall and this feeling came over me – it was like something took over my body, steering the van. It turned the van to the mall, parked and made me walk right to this health food store. I then started explaining to the clerk my struggles. I told her about my Crohn's, my daughter's health – she knew exactly what I needed. She grabbed this liquid Flora and said "Take this." My daughter was six months at the time but she assured me it was ok in smaller doses.

I decided to give it to my daughter and within twelve hours I saw a happier baby. This inspired me and I began to research Crohn's. I read the book *The Yeast Connection*, in the book it shared about the chlorine in swimming pools killing good bugs as well as bad bugs. Removing the good bugs left our bodies susceptible to yeast which causes diseases. Over time the yeast takes over and affects the weakened parts of the body. I had spent most of my summers in Montreal at the Glenmore swimming pool. My diet as a child was overcooked veggies, loads of meat, and tons of sugar. I had also been on antibiotics for over a two-year period for a reoccurring infection.

The Flora wasn't the whole answer.

When my youngest was four I took her off milk because she was developing asthma. The regular doctor told me to keep her on milk and give her a puffer. I had lost my trust in doctors because they didn't get holistic healing. My near-death had opened my view that we are part of the planet. There are herbs and plants that are there to heal our bodies, as well as the mind and spirit. This was in the early nineties before the holistic health kick of these days. I kept searching for more information and loved learning about this.

I read an article that my dear friend Juanita, who has since passed away, gave me about taking tea tree oil. The article was about bladder infections and the people in the pilot had taken tea tree oil for two months and healed reoccurring infections. I talked to a naturopathic doctor about taking tea tree oil, and he said I could take it, but only one or two drops on a full stomach. I also gave one drop to my youngest.

I took tea tree oil for two months and I no longer had symptoms of Crohn's. I bought books about herbs, other health books; anything I could get my hands on to learn as much as I could about natural healing. It made so much sense to me that the earth had the medicine we needed. I started taking ground ginger for inflammation and digestion, B6 for muscle spasms, and B12 for digestion. I drank chlorophyll in my water, and most importantly, took friendly bacteria and changed my diet.

My daughter stopped having asthma. She still had health issues, but was certainly better than she had been.

That was over twenty-five years ago and I am Crohn's and Colitis free to this day. I eat and drink whatever I want, in moderation of course. I don't take any medications for anything. I always use natural herbs and essential oils. I still research information on health issues. On YouTube there is the amazing Dr. Josh Axe and his friend Jordan Rubin who also suffered from Crohn's and Colitis and healed it naturally. These two have so much information about health and foods that are good for your body. I love them.

There are times when medications are necessary.

(Please do not follow this health information without professional advice from your doctor or naturopathic doctor. This is my story, not medical advice.)

TWELVE

Synapses

THINGS SETTLED in our new town. We became involved with a church, I felt it was a good thing for the girls. I felt that I had limitations as a mom because of my childhood experiences. I also knew I had not experienced good parenting and sometimes felt very confused about how to raise them. I knew it was important to surround them with good people to help raise them. I tried to be the mom that Mrs. C was for me. Having their friends over after school for tea. Listening to the girls, being there when they felt they were being bullied or had other troubles.

I was working for the school district at that time which was great. I saw so many kids' year after year go through the same issues, challenges, and behaviours. It gave me the insight that what my girls were doing was normal. I wanted them to have a good life.

The marriage was a challenge. We were arguing a lot. I believed that I was the problem, as I always did, so I decided to seek counselling.

I found out about a program from the government to pay for counselling for victims of a crime. I had reported Kathleen's abuse and had a case file number there, so we both were eligible for free counselling. That's when I met a Psychologist, Jane Wakefield. My angel. Jane saw Kathleen and I for over ten years.

Jane was an expert on Post Traumatic Stress Disorder. She gave me tools like EMDR (Eye Movement Desensitization and Reprocessing), Tapping, and other methods to release memories, rewrite them and heal the emotions from the past. Some of the things she had me do I thought were hokey, but they were working. I was letting go of past wounds and remembering more of my childhood. She worked on my timeline. If an issue came up, Jane fit me in.

There was a time when I could not stop crying. I was crying into a towel, bawling. I went to see Jane, and that was when I pulled up a memory and realized that I had been raped by my cousin. I had this memory of being on the ceiling, with the reflection of the leaves and looking at a light in the garden. Jane told me that I had had an out of body experience to deal with the trauma of the rape. She helped me work through the trauma and heal the wound.

I started using the techniques to do the releasing on my own. I was seeing more and more of the belief systems and memories that needed to be healed. I was very quick to let go of issues. My strong connection with my spirit gave me the strength to release without the fear of dying. The biggest fear I think people hold is the fear of dying, which I believe we learn during our first seven years. I didn't have a fear of dying, but I did have childhood fears like abandonment, rejection, etc.

I released too much in one day and I freaked myself out. I was now realizing how much of a lie my childhood was. The lies my dad taught me, the half-lies and half-truths he told me. How the whole family did a dance around the rage and dysfunction. There really weren't any relationships except codependency. Everyone in the family was reliant on everyone else to act a certain way to support the secret. The responsible older child, the rebel to act out and the younger to joke around and make the family laugh. We were taught it was our responsibility to take on our father's pain by acting out while living under his control.

I started to think, *What was real in my life then? Did my "reality" then only exist to protect my true reality from the secret?* To not know what was truth and what was a lie terrified me, and I began to panic. It became very clear to me that the only reality that mattered was the one I was in at this present moment. I had to keep my focus on exactly what was in front of me, the present moment, or I was going to have an emotional breakdown. I called Jane and she made space for me to come in. She helped me integrate the several disparate parts of myself. The parts that were broken through childhood fears and the adult part of me that was healing. I could feel myself becoming whole.

This time in my life was not too much fun for me. I had times when I wished I could go back to the "ignorant bliss" I was living in before, but not really. When was this crap going to end? I had to press on.

I began to question everything I believed and asked myself if it was true to me or not. I even found myself questioning how I put the dishes in the cabinet. My dad had controlled everything in my life through fear and I had no idea what I wanted.

I worked at two high schools and two elementary schools and was around kids of all ages. That helped my healing. It was like I was growing up with them in a way. I was learning new coping skills and the kids actually liked me. I thought I could make a difference in the kids' lives by connecting with them like Mrs. C and Mr. Saunders did.

I enrolled in a Certified Education Assistant program to work with special needs children. The psychology course was my favorite. I understood the course on a very deep level. I was seeing that I had a strong grasp of understanding people and relationships. I began connecting with teachers and building relationships with them.

There were a few challenging kids. One lunch we were heading into the school and one of my challenges called my name. I turned and he threw a basketball directly at my face. The ball hit my glasses and cut my nose. I reacted in anger and called him an asshole. I went in right away and told the principal what I had done. He was tolerant of me and suggested I find a better way to deal with those issues. At that moment, I was thinking, *Yes, but how?* It was like there was this block in me, in my brain, and I could see the block. There was a connection missing, this process of how to handle the situation without anger or reaction. What did that look like? I pushed my thoughts to get in touch with what that thought process was, what the next step was that I was missing.

I processed this for a few days – *If this happens, then what?* Or metacognitive thinking – I was becoming aware of what I was thinking or not thinking. I couldn't figure out what the next step was. I was reacting without thought. I had not learned strategies to deal with situations because of my fathers control, rage and family dynamics. All I knew was reacting and acting out in anger as my father had done. What could I do instead of reacting? As I processed these thoughts of what I could do next, I felt the front of my brain starting to tingle. It was like little sparks that were firing in my head. The sparks went on for a while. I was concerned.

I called the psychologist from the course I was attending, I knew she had done brain work with a doctor in the states. I told her what had happened, she said that a portion of my brain was firing up.

Synapses, she was not concerned.

I researched what the frontal lobe was responsible for and it made sense that I had not developed properly. My father had complete control of me and made all the decisions in my early years, so I had no need to develop that part of the brain. It was also the reason why I was not able to learn or be creative. The frontal lobe is responsible for problem solving, creative thinking, and logical thinking, among other things. I had lived all my life in the back lower part of my brain – in fear – flight, fright or freeze.

The more I healed, the more things were not going well in my marriage. We were never close on an intimate level and I was wanting more connection. I was working on my healing, believing that he was healed already and I was trying to meet him there. He had no interest in counselling or doing anything to save the marriage. He was being very distant, aloof, uninterested in me. I had been feeling ugly and unloved.

I started to see the patterns in my relationships and was asking myself why I was with him. I kept trying to talk to him about the issues to open his eyes. I didn't want the girls not to have a dad. I then discovered what was going on – he had an addiction.

I did an intervention and he decided to attend rehab. I was very hopeful. During his stay, he contacted his mom who helped him leave the rehab after twenty days, brought him home, and said he was fine. He stayed in his addiction and I worked on healing myself.

As the girls grew, I saw his addiction was not going to help them have a good view of themselves. I found his notes from rehab and realized how damaging the addiction was. I decided it was best that he left for the girls' sake.

Once again fear took over my life. Stress and chaos. Since my focus was not on the addict anymore, I began to drink wine in the evenings to cope.

I filed for custody of the girls and the on the day of court, he never showed up. I waited all day in the courtroom. When it came to our turn, the judge awarded me full custody. My lawyer said that he had never had that happen before, no show. The only visitation with the girls was to be supervised with a registered psychologist. I also received a restraining order. He had been harassing us.

The agreement was that I was to keep the house for the girls' sake and he kept the investments.

I focused on raising the girls, working two jobs (for the school district and cleaning houses), and being home for them. I did receive financial support from him, I was very thankful for that. It was a very challenging time for me, being mom and dad.

The ache in my soul was still there from my childhood. I had not come to terms with the fact that there was this ache, I had lived with it all my life. I hated being alone.

I ended up in another brief marriage with another addict.

My older daughter married.

It was time to sell the home and buy something more manageable than a third of an acre. I moved into a townhouse with my youngest. I loved the townhouse. My youngest was in high school, I had more time for myself. I bought a motorcycle and took riding lessons. I was trying to figure out who I was.

THIRTEEN

Online Dating

THERE I WAS in my late forties, single again, needy, lonely and desperate to be in a relationship. My girlfriend suggested I join the local dating site. I had never heard of such a thing. We sat down in front of my computer, eating popcorn and drinking wine, and created a profile on the site.

I had no idea what I was getting into. I uploaded pictures and information about myself that should have not been shared out into an unfiltered world. Within hours I had messages from so many men. It was overwhelming. I was naïve, vulnerable and a financial target. I never considered any of that. I was desperate to find someone to fill the void I was missing in my life, which was my own happiness, inner joy, acceptance of me and my own self-worth.

Within a few months I met a guy. He was charming, attentive, made me feel good. We were intimate very quickly. A few weeks later he sat down with me and discussed being exclusive. That we were *together*. He spoke about "trust." He went on, saying there had to be trust in the relationship, he said if the trust was gone the relationship was over. As I sat there listening to him, what he was saying became more confusing to me. I had always blindly trusted everyone whether they deserved it or not.

The next evening, he called me and talked to me about going to Mexico. He told me he had planned to go before he met me. I told him to go on his own, that I was not prepared to go to a foreign country with someone I had just met. The conversation carried on for forty-five minutes and he would not give up. He accused me of not trusting him. My head was hurting from the intense and confusing conversation – I gave in and agreed. The next morning, I received emails from him about where to go.

He decided everything and convinced me that two weeks was best. We made the arrangements and he insisted on putting the tickets on his Visa, and I could pay him back later. I didn't want to leave my daughter for two weeks, but I pushed down the feelings because he made me feel so special.

I had never been treated as well or had more fun in my life than when we were in Mexico. We met new people, hung around the pool and laughed. He was the life of the party and everyone loved him. When I dressed up he told me how beautiful I looked and walked proudly around the resort with me. I was hooked. I put him on a pedestal and questioned why this great guy would want to be with me. He was so popular and so charming.

My daughters and son-in-law did not like him, they told me he was very controlling. So, I went to his place in a nearby town three days a week to see him. I hate to admit that I was abandoning my youngest daughter. Leaving her alone those nights. I was so desperate not to be alone and so charmed by him. There was this unspoken sadness between my daughter and I.

He began to take control over me through his bullying rages and temper. If I did not what to do something he would become enraged with me. One time I told him I wasn't going on a motorcycle trip with him and he completely lost it with me. I thought he was such a great guy and blamed myself for his anger. I felt that if I tried harder and put him first he would not be angry at me. The relationship was so good at the start, I desperately wanted to keep having the good feelings and would do anything to keep it there. I had not dealt with my bullying issues as a child I did not understand what was happening between us.

I planned to move to the town he lived in before I met him. As my daughter's graduation came close I decided it was time to move. So, I put my townhouse up for sale. When it sold he offered for me to stay with him for the summer; to see how it would go being together. My daughter stayed with friends. My intuition was always telling me to run, but I convinced myself it was my issue, not him.

I wanted a new motorcycle – my smaller bike was not able to keep up with the Harleys. I mentioned this to him, and he took over my searching and decided what kind of bike I was going to buy. That pissed me off but I did not say anything, stuffed my feelings. He found the one he thought I should buy, but I told him I didn't have the money from the sale of the townhouse yet. He offered to lend me the money. I was surprised and it did not feel right. I said no. He told me that he trusted me with his money.

I took the bus to Medicine Hat with his cheque in hand. Thirteen hours away and arrived at 1 a.m. Climbing down from the bus I thought to myself, *What the heck am I doing?* There was only one cab and I shared it with a guy I didn't know. Completely out of my comfort zone. I checked into the hotel and went to bed.

In the morning, I went to pick up my bike. It was raining. I gave his cheque to the Harley shop, put my rain gear on and took off. I only made it 127 kilometres that day because of the rain. I arrived at Lethbridge, soaked to the bone. Went to the wine store, had dinner. We texted for a bit then I fell asleep.

The next day I woke up early and the sun was shining. I bought breakfast and took off down the road. I hit rain through the mountains – thank God it was not snow, it was only the end of May.

After thirteen hours of riding, I arrived at his place and he was not home. I thought it was very strange. I went to the pub that we hung out at. A friend of his was there and said to me, "I will see you there." I said ok and headed back to my boyfriend's place. No one was there. I decided to walk to the store and he pulled up in his car. He was very pissed at me. Apparently, he had planned a big arrival party at his work for me, with champagne and all his friends; but as my phone had died, I had no idea about the celebration.

Something in me was not sitting right. My spider senses kept going off, but in my mind, he was such a great guy. I would turn it back on myself and try to be better. I gave him the best cuts of meat, the last of the wine, the best of everything. I worshiped him.

A few months after I moved in with him, I told him that I was thinking of finding my own place. I felt better when I was on my own. I was missing my daughters and wanted them to feel welcomed. There was never any down time with him. Constant parties, friends, it was like a circus. I was finding myself in a brain fog, I didn't like the feeling.

While I was working at Costco he was shopping for real estate. He told me he was putting an offer on a property. I thought, *good for you*. He then invited me to go up to see the place, the next thing I knew I was being congratulated by the sales reprehensive about the purchase. He had made an unconditional offer on a property. I sat there in shock and very confused as she went through the contract. My name was on the contract! They had written his name in full **and/or** my first and last name. I never signed anything. Then she looked at me and asked me for the 10% down. $40,000. I was like, *what?* I said I didn't have $40,000 my money was invested. He then turned to me and said aggressively, "Well how much do you have?" I said, "Maybe $10,000." He then turned to the sales representative and asked her if that was enough to hold the place. She asked when would the remaining be paid. He turned to me and I said "I can't have anything before January." They changed the contract and she asked if we wanted 1 or 2 copies. He looked at me and said, "1 is fine." He took the contract and threw it in his trunk and I never saw it again. I couldn't believe what was happening.

The next morning, he left the house early, then called me and instructed me to take the cheque up to the property. I did what I was told. I became so stressed out and my stomach was upset all the time. He became very cold to me and I was living in shock. I was so confused, fearful of him. But I didn't see it! I thought he was such a great guy.

I kept bouncing between trusting him or trusting me. I realized that I had never trusted anyone since my childhood and we were now buying a half million-dollar place together. I made a conscious decision to trust him.

I noticed he was starting to cut me down in front of his friends. I called him on it and he became enraged. The relationship had changed.

I came to his place one evening after work and noticed all of my possessions piled up in the garage. These were special things that I had managed to keep all the years, sentimental to me. I asked him what he was doing and he told me that he was giving my stuff to a friend *in need*. I felt guilty and confused and let my special things go.

A few weeks later he demanded a letter from me about where the down payment came from for the property. I didn't understand what he was talking about and did nothing. A couple of days later he became enraged with me and told me he needed a letter for the mortgage broker to show where the down payment came from. That was when I began to realize something wasn't right. I thought, *You went to a mortgage broker with out me?*

He spent so much money on the new place, claiming he was building me "an oasis." $2000 BBQs, $1000 ceiling fans, granite, cherry wood floors, marble sinks, the list went on. When ever I suggested anything, or wanted something I was denied. The day we were to sign the papers at the lawyers, he asked me for a loan of $20,000 because he was short and told me he would pay me back. When I asked him for the money he informed me that he had gone over the bills and I actually owed him $10,000. When I asked him to see the bills, he refused.

After we moved in, I took pictures of my girls and put them on a mantle going down the stairs. I displayed them with a plaque with the word "Love" on it. I came home that night to see the pictures piled up and a candle holder in their place. I was devastated.

I was so depressed – constantly crying and couldn't figure out why. Here I was with this great guy, a new beautiful place, and I was so sad. I would stair out the window with tears streaming down my face.

I contacted Jane, the psychologist. We worked through my bullying issues with my dad. The threats my dad made to me and how I was so afraid of him. I released the emotional wound around the Valentine's Day party where I believed I was unlovable. I left her office feeling hopeful.

The next day we left for a road trip to Yellowstone National Park. As I was riding, I started to realize that I had people in my life that were bullying me now. I was frustrated with him that morning because everything was on his terms and time. I had no say in anything we were doing, every time I made a suggestion he would disagree. I saw his mood swings and his anger towards me. During our trip, we were at dinner one evening and he ordered lamb chops as an appetizer – I hated lamb and he knew it. He offered me one and I refused to eat it. Once again, he was pissed off at me.

I began to pay attention everything he was doing, the music he was playing like Lucinda Williams about being abused and used. At dinner he would start conversations about my relationship with my daughters and mother bringing up my emotional pain. I noticed the amount of wine he was pouring in my glass to keep me drunk. I was not liking what I was seeing and began to let him know. I thought if I let him know he would change. He just became anger and anger at me. I was still so confused.

Things fell apart very quickly after I saw what was going on. One afternoon he stated, "My relationships usually only last two years."

I remember thinking, *You bought a half-million dollar home with my money, with the intent of only being together two years?*

I made plans to leave without telling him. I took important papers like a copy of the purchase agreement, affidavits from his ex stating his anger and physical abuse towards her, other things that I thought would help me get my money back. I was shaking in my boots out of fear of him.

That's when I discovered that I was paying for all the bills and half the mortgage payment to him in cash. He demanded cash so his ex would not see it as income for support.

After I left him I gut-wrench cried for six months. I drank to numb the pain, I tried everything to get my money back. We ended up in court, and he knew the court system very well, better than me. I woke up in the middle of the night crying out to God, "What do I do?"

A very clear answer came to me: *WALK AWAY! He will keep you in a state of peril.* I walked away with $31,000, losing $187,000 of cash, with $25,000 of credit card debt.

I chose to trust him, just as I had trusted my dad a life time ago. My dad took advantage of my heart, my trust and violated me and now my boyfriend had done the same thing to me. I hit rock bottom. I had been stripped of everything, my possessions, my trust, my dignity; left raw, vulnerable and humiliated.

It wasn't over yet. He could no longer qualify for the mortgage on his own. He needed me to remain on the mortgage in order to stay in the home. I was homeless, penniless, lost everything and I had to keep him in the lifestyle he was accustomed to, using my money and credit. The situation was gut-wrenching. He refused to sell the house and I was still under his control financially. I couldn't qualify for a place or credit because of the mortgage. It haunted me.

I plugged along, trying not to think about the mess. I was living in blame, pain and pity. Felt devastated all the time. I was hired on with a real estate brokerage and held on the best I could.

I was living downtown and often found myself sitting at a pub with tears rolling down my cheeks. I was so confused and lost. The bar tender there was my angel, Dona reached out to me. There were times when I thought about ending my life and my angel helped me through it by being there for me.

I knew I wasn't doing well and contacted the Elizabeth Fry Society for counselling. Magdalena was assigned to my case. She was an eighty-year-old Spanish woman and was like a grandmother to me. She loved me, validated me and supported me. She gave me hope and nurturing. I wanted to become successful for her.

That's when I made a decision to get my real estate licence. I bought the books and started studying. I took a leap of faith that I was going to pass no matter what. I did the assignments and began to study the 1000 questions. Magdalena told me I was going to do great with this career. She often said that I didn't see my potential.

In November, I was laid off work and I gave myself four months to do a self-taught real estate course. Not once did I allow myself to think I couldn't do it. I went for it all in!

I would get up at 7 a.m., begin studying, and would take a break for breakfast. Get back at it again and study until dinner. I'd put my running shoes on, walk up the hill behind my place, bought wine, and went back home. I would do 100 questions a day. I set my date to write. February 2013.

I watched *SuperSoul Sunday* with Oprah to inspire me. There was this episode when she was interviewing Joel Osteen. They talked about his book, *The Power of I Am*. What resonated with me was this quote from Joel: "Whatever you say after "I am," it comes following you!" I searched for his sermon on YouTube, found it and watched it several times. Joel was speaking to me. I wrote sticky notes and stuck them all over my condo. It looked like I was schizophrenic. The notes were: I am successful, I am beautiful, I am strong, I am smart, etc. At first it was hard to say those things about myself, to myself. I kept repeating the words. I wore a blue elastic on my wrist to remind me of the positive words when I was out. I was determined to be successful.

The day before I wrote my license, I rode the bus to Vancouver. I studied all the way there. When I arrived in Vancouver, I went on the #14 to UBC campus, settled into my room, looked for where I was writing so I knew in the morning and found a local pub for dinner. I had a few glasses of wine and returned to my room. It was a restless night for me.

Time dragged the next morning. I was to write at nine and it felt like noon. When it was finally time, I put my earplugs in and I began to do the exam. I never even realized that everyone else was done before I was finished. I had absolutely no idea how I had done.

I stayed with my younger sister that evening. The next day when I was at the bus depot with my sister, I went on the website for the course, and there it was in red: "PASS." I couldn't believe it. I was ecstatic!! A rush of goosebumps came over me.

That exam was one of the hardest things I had ever done. And I passed.

I sold my first place sixteen days after being licensed. It felt good.

I was still very upset about losing everything to that man. I called the police to see if there was something I could charge him with. The police informed me that if I had not forced him to put my name on the mortgage and title I could have charged him with fraud. The very thing I did to save my money was a mistake. The police officer was very honouring. He sympathised with what I had been through. Congratulated me with my success in real estate. But the next line he said was the kicker: "However, you did write the cheque."

It took me a few days of playing those words over in my head to realize what the police officer said to me was true. I did give him the money. Yes, I felt bullied, I was living in fear of him, I couldn't see truth – however, I could have said, "No." My spider senses were yelling at me. I didn't listen to them. I made a decision to take responsibility for my actions. As much as it sucked to hear that from the police officer, he was right.

It was very humbling for me to own it even though it wasn't easy to do. What happened next was a surprise to me: I realized I was taking back my power. Owning what I did and reconciling with it actually felt good. My focus was no longer on him in the blame game, but me, and what I needed to do to get my financial and emotional power back.

The end of that year I truly took my financial power back. I sent him an email and told him that I was claiming bankruptcy. It wasn't true. He'd had enough time and was using my credit and money to build his financial portfolio. In the email, I apologized to him but said the house would be used to pay for the debt that I had incurred.

I quickly received an email back from him saying, "Let's meet and we can go over the debt and perhaps I can help you."

I thought, *What a ***************. I responded back that I would rather go bankrupt than have any part of him.

Within eight weeks he found the money and removed me from title and the mortgage.

I was finally free.

FOURTEEN

The Para-Dime Shift

WHILE I WAS STUDYING for my license I was seeing another guy.

The difference with this guy was that he triggered my pain and I was beginning to see it. We would get together maybe once a week, he was completely into me. Like we became one when we were together, no boundaries. Then when I left his place, I would feel alone and empty. I would become enraged and angry at him. I spent two years in and out of this relationship, trying to figure out what was going on.

I was still struggling financially and made a decision to move into the basement of a friend from the real estate office. It was cheap rent and I thought it was a good decision. The space was in a basement of a house, we were to share the kitchen. Because of the location of the house and being in a basement, my cell phone did not work very well, which wasn't good for my business.

There was so much going on in my emotional world. I was not getting ahead financially, I was in such a negative head space. Now that I was on my own, no kids to focus on or a full-time relationship, I was forced to face myself. I had used addictive relationships and wine to numb me out all my life. None of that was working anymore and the pain was getting stronger.

I lived in fear, which didn't make sense to me. This was the type of fear that started with a tingle in my lips. My heart would race, and the tingle would rage through my whole body, as if a lion was after me. When I thought about my financial situation, the fear would overcome me. I had never lived with credit card debt or lack of funds in my account. One day my managing broker said to me, "You look like a deer in the headlights. That is no way to do business, clients can smell fear a mile away." I went into my office with that said and sat at my desk. I knew he was right. In that moment, I made the decision to put my fear aside and get down to business. I put it aside but not away, promising myself that I would deal with the fear later. I focused on my inventory and began to sell.

I had never felt lonelier in my life. I was depressed, self-loathing, barely surviving.

I woke up with an ache in my soul every morning, feeling sorry for myself, lonely and angry, and actually scared. One morning the heaviness was particularly bad. I thought a powerwalk would help. I was sitting on the stairs putting on my shoes, and I noticed this dime in the corner, beside the dresser, on the floor. I had seen the dime several times before but never picked it up. I had wondered where it had come from. I was prompted to pick it up by my inner voice. I reached over, sat back down on the step, and looked at the dime in my fingers.

In that moment, this question came into my head: *Sara, what do you believe about yourself, that isn't true, that has created this mess?*

This dime brought me into the present moment. I thought about where I was living, and everything that was going on in my life– and realized I had created this life. There was this profound moment of realizing that I was responsible for everything. Right there and then I stepped out of the drama, out of the feelings and the thoughts and sat in the audience, just as I had done after my near-death experience. I realized it was time to start looking within for answers and stop believing that my pain would be lifted from the outside.

What did I believe that made me think I deserved this life? I would never have allowed this if I was still with my daughters. I would fight for them, why was I not fighting for me? Why did I not value me?

I went for a walk and made the decision to stop the pity party and pull up my socks. I needed to start looking at what I had hidden under the water all those years ago, and bring the emotions to the surface. Once again, I made a decision to accept where I was and take charge of changing my situation. What was I going to do about it??

That's when the universe started to respond. It wasn't easy to stay in the positive place but I kept trusting things would change. I found a 21-day meditation that Oprah was offering with Louie Schwartzberg and began to do the meditation. It moved me and reminded me of being in the light with the love, unconditional acceptance. The grace during my near-death experience. The wisdom from Louie also gave me insight into how I could live positively. I began to get excited to get up in the morning and receive the next day's meditation. Louie's photos were beautiful and they inspired me.

I found a new group of friends to hang out with. We would meet every Friday at The Train Station and socialized. The group was called "The Board Meeting." The leader of that group was a dear man. He reached out to me every Friday to give me wisdom and guidance. This one particular Friday I said these words to him, without thinking, "I don't care."

He looked me with his piercing eyes and said, "Excuse me Sara, you do care!" Those words hit me. He was right. Another needed kick.

I was awkward at the gatherings. I realized that I did not have any social skills or ability to read social cues. I began to watch people that I admired and mimicked their words and actions to teach myself these skills. I was still dealing with insecurities and feeling bad, but I was determined to get my life together.

One Friday, this lovely lady sat beside me. She was sharing this event she was attending. It was a fundraiser for breast cancer. She was ziplining for breast cancer – the catch was, she was ziplining topless. She turned to me and I thought she was going to ask me for a donation. I was thinking, *I am broke.*

She said, "You should come do it."

Without hesitation, I said "Yes." I knew I was meant to do this. I used to do risky things like scuba dive and ride a Harley. I had lost that adventure in me, it was time to renew that adventurous side.

I had recently reconnected with a friend on Facebook who was fighting a battle with cancer and the double negative gene, the same as Angelina Jolie. I shared the event details with her. The next thing I knew, she was heading up to Peachland to zipline with seven friends and the CTV news crew. They were doing a three-part series about her battle, and this event was now part of her story.

Finding sponsors was not difficult when I told men what I was doing! I quickly earned my $150 to enter.

It was becoming obvious that there had been this big shift in me after finding the dime and the meditations. I was beginning to take responsibility for my own reality and for creating positive things. I also began to see how much the universe was guiding me. I decided to buy more meditation CDs from Oprah and Deepak to keep myself in "my place of grace."

I was starting to share my near-death experience with more people. A friend gave me the book *Dying to Be Me* by Anita Morjani, which reminded me of my near-death experience. The book encouraged me to think about writing my journey to share with others.

The dime was very important to my financial belief system. I was trying to understand why I had such limiting beliefs about money. Why some people seemed to have it land on their lap and some struggled so much to receive it. I had so much potential to make such great income with my business, but I wasn't. I asked the universe to show me why it was this way for me and I had a "para-dime shift."

I started to dig into my memories about money. I remembered my Dad saying quite often after the bills were paid, "We only have a dime left over." I remembered asking for money for school supplies and field trip money, which were basic needs. I was always very careful that my mom was in a good mood before I asked her for money. I had so much guilt about needing money and being terrified to ask for it. Money was my mom's way of feeling she had some control over her life.

I never felt I deserved anything good.

It was time for me to start trusting the universe again. I did have blind trust in the world as a child, even though I was in pain. I always saw the cup half full. It was important to find that trust in me again. Before I lost everything, I did see the good in people, and trusted that, even though it was an untrue filter. I had consciously made a decision to trust my boyfriend and not myself, as I had done with my Dad. Trusting what was familiar, what I was taught to trust – abusive people. It was me I needed to trust – my gut, my spider senses – and trust that the universe was on my side.

FIFTEEN

Letting Go

THE DAY CAME to go ziplining, the weather was horrible. It was raining and cold, however I headed to the zipline. I was thinking of the women who were facing the war with breast cancer – what was a little rain? As I was driving a song began to play: *You are So Beautiful to Me* by Joe Cocker. This song was so fitting for the day, which I didn't realize at the time.

I arrived at the site. There were newspaper crews taking pictures and interviewing us, it was a little weird. My friend from Vancouver and her van full of friends drove up. They were dressed in pink craziness. Another van pulled up and Tamara Target, from the Vancouver news, came out of the van. They were there to film the story. I had no idea how big this was.

It was time to get ready. We went into one of the two tents, then we stood behind a harness and we all started to take our clothes off. It was very awkward. Some ladies only took their tops off, some went completely naked. I thought, *Why not go all in, completely naked?* As I took off my clothes I had this moment. There were large ladies, thin ladies and my friend who had one breast standing together – we were all so different, yet each of us were beautiful, brave and courageous.

All of us were being open and vulnerable to each other. Perfect in our own unique way.

We put on the harnesses, wrapped ourselves in the blankets, and made our way to the platform. That was when it really hit me – what exactly was I doing? I hated heights, and I was naked! I watched each lady ahead of me going up to the platform. For each person, the attendant would take the latch that was attached to the harness, hook it to the reel, and then off she would go.

Before I knew it, I was on the platform. I sat back, fought the fear and trusted, then took a leap of faith. There I was screaming down the line above the tree tops, I thought, *This is pretty cool*. I felt like a bird flying through the air. I was hanging on to the rope attached to the line for dear life, then I thought to myself, *Let go*, and I did. I flew in the air with my arms and legs stretched out. Screaming, butt-naked and free.

When I landed on the platform, I was transformed. It was so exhilarating and uplifting. I was so excited to go on the next one, back to the other side. I didn't want to quit, but that day there were only the two lines open.

When I headed home, all I wanted was someone to share the experience with. I wanted to debrief, share my excitement. I had no one to talk to, so I went to a local pub. When I walked in there was the leader of "The Board Meeting" having a beer. This was not our usual pub and it was a surprise to see him. He looked at me and said, "You don't have any idea how much this has changed you." You are a new person." I knew something had shifted.

It took a few days to realize that I had faced three of my biggest fears. My body image, my fear of heights, and my feeling of being inferior to other women. There I was, bonding with all sixty-two ladies. Standing up for each other, in it together. That was perfection.

I believed I was doing this for a friend and I received the bigger gift: I let go.

A few weeks later, I was forced to come to terms with my debilitating fear. The one like a lion was chasing me.

I was sitting having my morning coffee on the couch in the "dungeon," when an altercation broke out upstairs, with angry voices and yelling. Fear rushed over me and I flashed back to my father's rage – him throwing things and yelling at my mother, and my mother yelling back. My sisters and I fleeing to the basement, sitting there terrified. The fear of never knowing if my mom was going to still be alive when it was over. There was one particular time when I grabbed the phone and called 911. I quickly hung up out of fear of what I thought my father would do to me if the police showed up.

That was the fear.

That terrifying fear like a lion was chasing me. I sat there and went back to the memories. I would come upstairs to see what damage was done to the house. I would pick up the mess and clean, while my mom licked her wounds and my father pranced away in his egotistical way. I knew I had to release the energy around that fear. I had lived in fright or flight all my life, it was actually how I made all of the decisions about my life for a very long time. That had to stop.

Shortly after this breakthrough of realizing what the fear was, I knew it was time to move from this space. It was no longer where I was meant to be – I had learned what I was meant to learn. My thinking process had shifted. I was now realizing that everything – events, friends, relationships, and circumstances – was about my beliefs. Hidden from the consciousness but showing up in my world. I was beginning to see that every event was an opportunity to heal myself or understand myself better.

It was time to take a leap of faith in my finances.

I mentioned to a friend I wanted to move, and she said that she had a space in her home that I may want to rent. This time I went and looked at it, and the space was beautiful. It was bright, with a kitchen, and not on a hill. It was more money than I thought I could afford, but I said, "Yes." I loved it and so I moved in.

I started to thank people from my past, for the lessons I learned from them and the realization that they were all gifts for my healing. I was even becoming grateful for giving my house and belongings away so that I could hit rock bottom, face my truth and become me again. This was an evolving view; there were moments when I found myself back in the pity party place, but I quickly remembered it was a gift. I was training myself to be responsible for me.

SIXTEEN

The Flood Gate

DURING THIS TIME, as I mentioned before, I was seeing a fellow. He was very intelligent and had a lot of sales experience. Once again, like all my other relationships, I felt inferior to him, put him on a pedestal and worshiped him, without realizing it at the time.

He did teach me a lot and I am grateful. When we talked, I listened to his thinking process. The way he explained things, his outlook on life, and how he looked out for his best interests, both personally and professionally.

During this time, I was considering moving brokerages because I was having challenges with going from administration to realtor in the same office. I went to him to discuss my dilemma. I was worried about everyone's feelings and couldn't process what to do. It took a week of discussion before I finally saw his point of view. What was best for me and my business? I had never really thought of it that way before. I always put everyone else's feelings first. This was very enlightening. He walked me through problem solving, opened me up to thinking.

When I was with him, I was completely immersed in him. It was twelve hours of intensity, then I would go home and feel depressed, not knowing why. I would become intensely angry at him. Raging and sending spewing emails and texts. I couldn't figure out what was going on. I tried to break up with him for two years, but I never could receive closure.

I decided to hire a life coach who I had met at the Friday Board Meetings. We met one morning and chatted for an hour. He asked me this question: "Tell me what your Disneyland looks like?" I sat there in awkward silence, having no idea what he meant. I never ever had dreams, hopes. As a kid, I was living in hopelessness, with no escape. Dreams were a luxury for the chosen people, not for me.

I really had no idea that I had this challenge. I had lived like a pinball in the drama. Flight or fright making the decisions for me. My coach shared with me that its important to visualize to create your reality the way you want it. So, we began a year-long journey together, working on my path. Learning how to visualize. The first thing he had me do was go to the store and look at what I was planning to purchase, with my $20,000 a month income. He had me allocate where that income was going to be spent: savings, investments, spending, short term savings and charity. I planned for thirty months.

I started to become aware of the emotional abuse that I had been subjected to all my life through all my relationships. How I allowed myself to be controlled by men. How I have never felt safe through out my life. I truly valued having my coach to support me and help me heal.

I spent a lot of time searching for inspiration on YouTube. TED talks were one of my favorites. I discovered the short videos by Brendon Burchard that were very uplifting and so positive. I ordered his book *The Motivation Manifesto* from Chapters and watched a few videos a day.

I started my morning with Oprah and Deepak's 21-day meditations. My favorite was "Manifesting Grace through Gratitude." Their words had a way of reconnecting me back to my spiritual self. The meditations reminded me of that "place of grace" that I had been in during my NDE. The unconditional love, complete acceptance and peace.

I lived in that place for a year then found a new place downtown near the lake. I found a core group of friends, which was very comforting. They became family to me.

The day before the twenty-seventh anniversary of my dad's death I was searching the internet and YouTube for things to watch and learn. I discovered an amazing woman, Yvonne Oswald, PhD. Yvonne was sharing how her hypnosis strategy could heal multiple personalities, trauma, and many other challenges. I was very interested in seeing what she was about and watched a few of her interviews. Yvonne invited me to her website www.globalwelcome.com. I went on her site and downloaded an offering, "Sunshine-thinking" Track 1. In the hypnosis Yvonne takes you back in time, to before you are born. I decided to do the hypnosis that day. After I had a lovely sense of calmness but not much else.

The next morning, I woke up and did my usual morning sit on the couch with a coffee to check in and see how I was feeling. My thoughts went back to my childhood and OMG!! I could feel **ALL** my childhood emotions. The emotional floodgate had opened. I felt my feelings for my dad, how my heart ached. My feelings for my mom – it was like being outside the house and looking through the window to see the feelings. I was trying so hard to make them happy. I felt so burdened and sad. There I was, feeling it all, all the pain. I began to cry, and I cried and cried and cried. I had never cried like that before. I gut wrench blubbered for hours. Then the anger took over me. I yelled at my dad how angry I was. I punched pillows, yelling, "How could you dad?" I cried and yelled until the wee hours of the morning.

I released so much pain that I was extremely vulnerable for weeks. I had to cross my arms in front of me to protect myself from people's emotions and energies. I was open and raw. Having the emotions hidden under the water, safe and protected, was one of my coping mechanisms. I realized I had to now needed to protect myself from other peoples' feelings, it was not my responsibility to take the on. It was ok not to take on other peoples' issues. Wow, what a freedom!

I also realized that I had never trusted my intuition. I always had this knowing when something was not right, but didn't act on it. In fact, I seemed to be drawn to the danger. My spider senses screamed when I was a child that what my dad was doing to me was wrong. But he loved me. Here was my dad, the one who I thought would protect me as I was lying on his chest all those years ago… then having him turn around and use that vulnerability and trust to violate me to the depth that he did. He used the trust and guilt to manipulate and control me, teaching me to treat myself with such disgust.

After releasing that layer of emotion, a new level of feelings came to surface. I was out with my friends drinking wine and contacted the fellow I was seeing. He picked me up and I spent the night with him. The next morning, we had breakfast together as usual. Then we sat in conversation for the next few hours – however, this time I became very aware of what was going on between us. I began to realize that I did not really like the way I felt when I was with him. He actually stressed me out!

He dropped me off at home. I immediately began to feel this emotional pain. I had not been aware of it before. I stayed with the pain, deciding to figure out what I was feeling. The feeling was gut-wrenching. My intuition was telling me to do the hypnosis CD from Yvonne again, so I did. After that I did the technique that Jane gave me to take the emotion back into my memories to see what came to me.

This is what I remembered. There I was, sitting on the couch looking out the window. I may have been four. I was watching for my dad. He was late again and my mom was angry. I sat there with such fear and abandonment. I was terrified he would not come home. I lived completely through my dad, so felt I was surely going to die without him. That was how my four-year-old mind had processed my life. I lived with this deep gut-wrenching fear of being abandoned by my father all my childhood, which then spilled into all my other rela-tionships. This was why I always had to have a man in my life. I would feel the abandonment and empty when I was alone.

The next memory that came to me was when my dad had completely rejected me after he stopped abusing me. He refused to validate me or even have a relationship with me. He had no more use for me. I had been living through him all those years, I was his special one, then nothing. He turned around and left the family shortly after that. The rejection was the second part of the feelings. I released the emotional damage with this memory and released the rejection.

It was another big day.

This guy I was with now was just reinforcing my feelings of rejection and abandonment. Then I would send emails and texts to him, spewing out my anger towards him. The relationship was full of chaos and it had come down to random booty calls, which reinforced my lack of self-respect. It was not positive for either of us and I began to end it. We did have fun together, which was hard to give up, but I didn't feel I was respecting myself by seeing him anymore.

SEVENTEEN

Forgiving Myself and Taking Back My Personal Power

EARLIER IN THIS book I shared the beginning part of my Near-Death Experience which was very dark and evil. The dark horrific place that was calling me. I began to spend time trying to sort out what that part of the experience was about. The movie *Ghost* with Demi Moore and Patrick Swayze has a scene that is pretty close to the feeling. After Patrick killed his murderer, horrid screaming ghosts come to get the spirit of the murderer. Patrick's reaction says it all. I recalled the gut-wrenching pain of my experience with that scene. I didn't tell people about this part of my near-death for a long time because I was afraid of it. I was not able to face the truth of that part of the experience because I was still emotionally living in fear and pain in my life.

As I healed my childhood fears I was able to think about that part of the near-death experience and share more about it. I realized that the dark place was what I believed about myself. I decided I was evil after looking in the mirror as a child and realizing my eyes were the same colour as my dad's. I was carrying the belief that I was responsible for causing all of my family's pain and fears. The deep-rooted guilt that it was all my fault.

When I was in the darkness I asked for forgiveness and I immediately went to the loving light. I was asking myself and God to forgive me for believing the fear and pain were my truth. My near death taught me that what I was believing about myself was not true and I needed to forgive myself.

One of the pivotal points in my forgiveness walk was when I heard Oprah's favorite quote from her dear friend Maya Angelou, "When you know better, you do better." When I heard this quote, it spoke to me. Peace came over me when I realized that I had done the best I could over all those years, with what I had been taught and the tools that I had. I kept repeatedly thinking back, wishing I had done things differently, especially with my girls. But now I realized how beating myself up was not supporting where I wanted to be in my life.

I met with my girls and asked them to forgive me for my limitations as a parent, and the pain I had inflicted on them. This was when I realized that perhaps I was not supposed to be a perfect parent. Maybe what they went through was exactly the way it was meant to be, so they too would seek their spiritual truth and their life purpose.

I spent so much of my life kicking myself about things I did and trusting the wrong people, especially when I didn't trust myself, my spider senses. How many times did I look back over my mistakes (or gifts) of the past, being in the healing place I was in now, and say to myself, *How could I have been so stupid?* Hindsight. Why was I taking the lessons I learned through the mistakes and my healings, then going back to my past where I could see what I had done wrong, and kicking myself again? It was important to feel grateful for the lessons. I wouldn't be where I was now emotionally without those gifts.

I blamed myself for the abuse for a long time. I recalled my childhood many times during my healing with anger and guilt, believing that I was the one causing the abuse and creating the family pain. Then someone said to me, "You were only three." I made some excuse, came back to a similar point, and then they said it again: "You were only three!" You had a right to trust your dad, it was not your fault." At that moment, I thought of my granddaughter with her innocence and trust. How she would hold my hand, believing with all her heart that I was her protector. I saw myself in her. For the first time, I got it, let myself off the hook and forgave me.

All the decisions that I had made and things I did were based on what I had learned growing up. The most important thing now, was that I was doing something about it. I was working on my healing. It was important to be kind to me and give myself the unconditional acceptance and the grace that I had been given when I was in the light.

I also saw how important it was to forgive others, which helped me forgive myself. During this process, I wondered what had happened to my parents as children. Who taught them to live in fear? What had happened to them to act out the way they did? After thinking about them this way and understanding them more I thought, *Perhaps they were perfect parents for my spiritual walk and my life's purpose*! This view gave me peace in my heart towards them and allowed me to see good things about my parents. This was another level of taking back my personal power. I was no longer blaming myself or feeling like a victim of my parents' abuse, but taking responsibility for how I wanted to live my life.

It was a process and it was not always easy to feel the pain I was living in, believing it was my purpose. However, I leaned in and let my parents off the hook.

EIGHTEEN

More Dimes

I ALWAYS KNEW that I was meant to write a book. I would think, *Who me? The person that was reading at a grade two level in grade seven? I don't have anything to say.* As I worked through my childhood issues and began to feel confidence, I started to think, *Why not?*

As my view shifted about writing, I began finding more dimes. There was the first one I found while living in the basement that completely shifted my perception of my life. Now there were dimes on the sidewalk, dimes as I was walking downtown. Dimes between two Lamborghinis. These dimes were clean, as if they had just been dropped. It became very apparent that someone was trying to get my attention – perhaps my grandmother.

As I became more aware that I was meant to write a book, I decided to attend a local three-day workshop about telling your story by speaking up and writing: "Shine Live" by Chantelle Adams. This was an event with 120 women from all walks of life. I had done the workshop the year before as well, but at that time I had just hid in the back of the room, feeling less than and inferior to the other women.

This time I was going to be present and sit up front. I made an effort to sit at new tables and meet new women. It was uncomfortable – I hid my feelings from them, and I pushed forward. I stepped out of my discomfort and shared my feelings with one of the ladies there. She informed me that she and many of them felt that way and it was ok. That surprised me because I thought it was just me!

On the third day of the event I missed the morning. I was showing properties to a friend. When I finished showing the properties to her, I crossed the street to return the keys. I stepped between two Lamborghinis and there on the ground between them was a dime. I picked it up, all shiny and new. I turned to people on the street and told them with delight, "I have now found thirty dimes!"

I arrived at the event just before lunch. The seats were limited, there was one right up front and I sat down. There were five ladies there sharing about fears and limitations they had in their lives. Shortly after sitting down my phone rang, it was regarding a real estate deal I was working on. I went outside the building to talk. I looked at the ground and noticed it had rained. There was a business card on the ground upside down that was getting wet. I thought, *That looks like my business card.* After hanging up the phone, I bent down to pick it up. Guess what? There was a dime right beside it!! Number 31!!

OMG, I was elated. I went back into the event and sat down and showed the dime and the card to the ladies at the table. One of them said, "Oh yah, I saw that dime but I knew it wasn't for me." I couldn't believe it! I had only given my card to one lady the day before. Where did it come from? Was the universe telling me that I was supposed to be there at this event??

That afternoon one of the speakers was an author. She was presenting her program to the women about writing a book. She asked a question, "How many of you want to write a book?" Everyone put up their hand. Then she asked, "How many of you have thought about it for the past five years?" About a third of the women put up their hands. Then she asked, "How many of you have thought for your lifetime that you were meant write a book? Please stand up." About eleven of us stood up, including me, and she said, "You now have over 100 witnesses, go write your book!"

I said "Oops" out loud and everyone started to laugh.

That's when I decided to work with a new business coach on the outline of my book. I shared a bit of my journey with him about my abuse. This was new to me, sharing my story with such detail. He became emotional at one point. He looked down, shook his head and said, "I hate your dad." That validation from him touched my heart and gave me a sense of value. I was very moved by his feelings. However, I told him that I had forgiven my dad, he had done the best he could with what he knew. When I left his office, and walked towards my car, I looked down, there on the ground was another shiny dime.

I have shared my dime journey with many of my friends. There are so many people who have dime stories. One of my friends quoted to me, "Life can turn on a dime." Mine sure did!!!

NINETEEN

Nothing Is by Accident

IN NOVEMBER last year I began to write because I needed to figure out why I was still attracting bullies into my life. The bullies were not like my dad but like the ones I had been subjected to in school all those years. The year started with me being bullied and humiliated by a peer. Then I attracted 3 bully male clients that were horrible to me. The final straw was when a female friend tried to take me down. That was when I thought, *enough*. I was emotionally spent and decided to write to try and figure out why I was attracting these people into my life. Then the hopelessness and worthlessness came up for me which I wrote about in chapter 3, I took a three month break from writing.

In February this year I met a friend regarding some business I was doing with her, and she asked me how the book was coming along. I told her that I had taken a break, which started me thinking it was time. I began to write again.

I picked up where I left off and began to write. As I wrote there were more feelings welling inside of me. I was feeling burdened. Heavy-hearted and very negative again. This one particular day I took a break from writing and declared the day to be a mental health day to give myself some time to process. I was reading posts from friends on Facebook when I came upon a post for the Louise

Hay's movie, *You Can Heal Your Life*. I clicked on it and started watching. I completely identified with the woman in the story. This movie showed me that my inner voice was nasty, negative and self-defeating. The movie spoke to me so much that I watched it twice that day. At 3 p.m. I was still in my housecoat, definitely a mental health day.

Louise Hay's personal story really resonated with me. I identified with her story of abuse and how she had not developed social skills until she met her husband. She was now a successful best-selling author and mentor. I thought, *"Why not me?"*

I went onto Louise Hay's website and found her 101 daily affirmations and downloaded it onto my phone. I put on headphones and listened to them while I went on a 10K walk to the store. At first it was difficult to hear the affirmations. My inner voice was very negative, which I never realized before.

The next morning, I was on Facebook again and there was an ad for Dr. Michael Bethwith's mastermind. I was very drawn to this ad, as I had seen Michael being interviewed about one his books by Oprah on *SuperSoul Sunday*. His teachings resonated with me during the interview. I watching the mastermind that was about living your purpose. Towards the end Michael did a meditation prayer, about "healing in my bones." I was moved. My mood had lifted and I felt lighter, more open, and clearer in my mind.

Michael talked about living our purpose on this earth. I thought back to my near-death when I was at the crest of the light and was asked if I really wanted to die, and I said, "No, I have to go back and do what I was meant to do."

That night I was dreaming very dark dreams and woke up panicking several times. I couldn't figure out what was bothering me again. I had a meeting the next morning and thought I was anxious about it. I was driving to the meeting I feeling dread and insecurity, *Why do I have to do this?* I thought to myself, *Sara, choose confidence.* It made me feel a little better. I tried to imagine myself in the meeting feeling strong. It didn't work.

I became very aware of the insecurity and negative chatter in my head. I felt as though everyone could see I was a fraud. Everyone else had their lives together and mine was a mess!

That night I had a dream about my sister and I. I let her down in the dream and once again was not there for her. There was this sense of guilt. I was carrying the heaviness in my heart. I woke up several times in the night with that panic again. In the morning, my heart was so heavy. I knew it was time to do something about the feeling. I went to my meditation spot. I asked my higher power to help me understand what this was. I could not identify the feeling. What first came to me was guilt – I had felt so guilty for not being there for my sister – but it went deeper than that. I did the technique Jane had taught me years ago and went back into feeling to recall the memory.

I went back into this deep-rooted pain. I recalled this memory of coming home after being with my boyfriend when I was fifteen, loathing myself. There I was, sitting in the bathroom on the toilet lid, with my head in my hands. I felt so ashamed of myself for having sex with him. Disgusted. Ugly. I felt that through my last relationship too. I leaned into the memory and pain. I went into the feeling and asked myself what I needed to do to release this. I had been acting out the only thing I knew to get rid of the pain I was in, just as my dad had taught me. I sat in this process for a while and I could feel this release in the pit of my stomach.

Then I realized that the guilt and shame that I was carrying was his, not mine. He must have believed that he was flawed too. Then these words came to me: "Toxic Shame." OMG that was what that feeling was. This deep-rooted belief that I was flawed, that there was *something wrong with me* at the core of my being.

I had been living with this belief all my life. That I was flawed, not that I did something wrong but *I was wrong*. I was living under this belief, this pain trying to be normal, without understanding any of it.

I released the Shame on a cellular level, the pain in my gut was gone and this sense of calmness and peace came over me. Then all of a sudden, I felt this excitement bubble up and out of me from my gut. I was so relieved, I danced around my place saying, "Yes! Yes! OMG." I knew this was big! The core issue I had been wanting to heal forever. I called my girlfriend and told her what had just happened. I was ecstatic….

I really wanted to understand "Toxic Shame." I went onto the computer and googled "effects of toxic shame." I found a blog on "Psychology Today" which described my childhood exactly: being constantly ridiculed, shown I had no value except for pleasing my parents, take on their shame, yelled at, treated as though I was worthless. To survive in my world, I had no choice but to take on the shame and see my dad as my God.

This was also why I ended up in abusive relationships. I would put men with toxic shame on a pedestal, they were perfect in my mind and believing that I was flawed. This belief, along with rejection, abandonment, being bullied, and carrying the responsibility for everything, kept me coming back to abusive men. The pain I would feel when I was alone was gut-wrenching because I was carrying their pain as well. These men would reinforce the belief I was bad by emotionally abusing me and continuing the cycle. I kept thinking that if I were a better person, the relationship would go back to the honeymoon stage. The ironic thing was, while I kept trying to fix myself in order to be better in these relationships, these efforts actually became the catalyst to keep me searching - to heal myself, and move me forward to a healthier life.

Over the next few weeks, I was seeing how much this belief that I was flawed had affected every area of my life. I was always looking over my shoulder, hoping no one would find out that I was a fake. The shame blocked me from any chance of having a good relationship. My focus was to numb out this bad feeling any way I could. I would make bad choices in the evening to escape the pain, such as over drinking or gambling or sex with someone, then wake up in the morning, beating myself up verbally in my head for the behavior. This behavior would only reinforce the toxic shame that I believed to be true, then I would repeat the cycle again. Destructive, addictive behavior that kept me isolated and alone.

I began to look at every area of my life to see where this toxic shame was affecting it. This was why I was attracting bullies into my life. I was giving out a feeling that I was inferior, less than, with a target on my heart. The takers in the world could feel this and would take. Toxic shame had affected every area of my life!

Letting go of the shame was the first part of the puzzle. The next was noticing the stress I was creating in my life. That was why I was having panic attacks. I kept sabotaging my finances, my goals, and many other areas of my life, then would wake up freaking out, overtaken with worry. I often wondered why I had these attacks, because I really did know that my higher power had my back. When I trusted; everything worked out. I had been so guided and kept asked myself, *Why do I keep falling into worry and panic?*

Once again, I sat down in my spot and I went back to a memory of when I was probably five years old. I was in bed terrified; my mom was sitting on the edge of the bed. I was asking my mom, "Are you and dad going to get a divorce?" I had no idea what divorce meant but I knew it was bad. My mom looked puzzled and asked me where I had heard that word from. It was rare that people divorced in those days. My dad had threatened me with that word to keep the secret. My mom assured me that it wasn't going to happen but I carried this terrified burden that something bad was just around the corner. That was when I took on the emotional responsibility of the family – I needed to carry this secret to keep the family together. I began to act out by stealing, lying, and causing issues to keep everyone focused on me and not on the truth. The stealing also gave me a rush because I got away with it, and it gave me a sense of power. Then guilt and shame of this behavior would support my belief that I was bad, that would compound my pain. Even though I was an adult I was still acting out the same learned behavior. Keeping the chaos and the focus on me. This was another huge part of healing!

I had released that gut-wrenching ache in my soul!!

It took me a few weeks to really start to understand what I had done. I felt very uncomfortable with this new peace in my life. I was waking up in the morning with no negative talk in my head. When I was out with my friends, I was having intelligent conversations and sharing my opinions. The conversations were becoming deep and meaningful. When I met strangers, I was comfortable with them and began conversations that were very meaningful. My energy had also changed and I was attracting different kinds of people around me. I realized that the toxic shame had been keeping me isolated and alone, even in a crowd.

This was quite a change for me.

I had never realized how selfish I was being with my friends and daughters. I was looking at people in my world to make me feel better and I never asked how people were doing in their life with authenticity. There was always this block stopping me from feeling empathy or care on a deep level. I did care but it was selfish, I more wanted them to make me feel better. All of a sudden, I am asking people how they were, and I really want to know. It is an honor to give love and understanding to them. This was a very strange feeling but it was good.

It was my job to just Love the way I was loved in the light. The unconditional acceptance of each person for exactly who they were regardless of what was going on in their lives. To do all I could to support them (not rescue them) to be the best they could be. I was becoming able to see people beyond their behaviors, who they really were and to just love them.

I began sharing things I was seeing without much thought. My dear friend Bob showed me that I had to be careful. I would say something to someone or ask them questions and he would say to them, "How do you like being analyzed?" He was right!! I had to be careful with what I said and wait for the tap on the shoulder. Not everyone was ready to hear what I had to say!

I could see that toxic shame caused an enormous barrier between the authentic me and the world. I can see this barrier is the difference between love and fear. I believe this is why people do horrible things in this world, to reinforce what they believe about themselves – that they are broken, flawed or even evil – which isn't true. Remember the darkness before the light in my Near-Death Experience! The darkness I saw was what I believed about myself, not what God believed!

TWENTY

What an Incredible Journey

WRITING this book has been so incredible for me. As I wrote about one event, there was a release to allow another layer to come out. I have healed a depth of wounds that I had no idea were there to heal. I see how writing even the first layer would help so many of us holding on to emotional baggage. Without realizing what I was doing, I held on to my story so I could reinforce the negative belief system I had about myself and keep me in my pain.

I started to write this book to help other people heal and ended up healing myself!

My NDE reconnected me to my spirit, to my place of grace, but I was also living in such emotional pain caused by earthly experiences. I often thought that perhaps I was bipolar. There were times when I was completely in the physical world ridden by fear and then completely in the spiritual world with love, without much balance in between. By healing the emotional wounds, letting go of beliefs that were not true, and finding what my truth was, I now live in a balanced place. The present moment.

It was necessary to put myself in these situations with all their drama, then step back into the audience and learn from them. This process was paralyzing at times; there were moments when I wished I had stayed in "ignorant bliss." But however safe that ignorance of what was really happening in my life may have felt comfortable for me, it wasn't an option, thank God. I dreamt for the day that I would have peace in my life and to be honest, many times I wasn't sure if it would be possible.

I love looking back at my whole journey and seeing how each part was instrumental to my healing.

This is the process I go through to heal the energy that is attached to the emotion that I want to release and let go. (This technique is for releasing Post Traumatic Stress.) I am sharing this with caution. I advise you to get professional help to go through this process. The shifts can be overwhelming and traumatic in themselves.

The first step is becoming aware of the behavior or emotion that you want to change. This can be through some feelings from a dream, a flashback or a trigger. Step back out of your thoughts and emotions, you are the one experiencing them. It's like being in "the audience" or your spirit and be aware of what you are feeling.

Find a quiet place to sit, in your own space, where you will not be disturbed. Take your dominant hand's ring finger and thumb and pinch the top of your nose. The other two fingers will naturally touch the "third eye" of your forehead. Leave them there. Then take the other hand and place it on the back of your head and the base of the skull. Close your eyes and ask yourself to show you what memories the emotions are attached to. Your brain will take you there to a memory. These memories or behaviors are quite often from your first seven years of your life where you felt everything. This was before your cognitive thinking was developed. It could be a trauma that you experienced years later, like me panicking on the operating table.

Sit in the feeling for a while and ask yourself what you need to do to heal it. I tend to keep my head tilted towards the ground. You will figure it out, there is no wrong way, it's your way. When a memory comes up ask yourself how to heal it. I remember going back to the first time I was touched inappropriately by my father. When I went back to heal the trauma with this process, this is what I did. The big me walked into the bathroom of my childhood house. There I was, my child-self standing on the counter, and my dad putting cream on my skin after a bath. I walked up to him, grabbed him (the adult me) and punched him in the face. I watched him as he fell into the bathtub, hitting his head on the tile. I then went up to the little me, covered me with a towel, held me in my arms. I brought me home to myself to keep safe from harm. I then spent the next few weeks with a visual of little me being in a snuggly with me. I then integrated little me into big me through another process jane taught me.

Once you feel that you have let go of the emotion and feel peace about the memory, move on to the next step. Your body had held onto these emotions on a cellular level, which I believe causes illnesses. It is important to accept the new memory, the healing, on the cellular level.

Take your hands and put your fingers around your ears, your thumbs at chin level. Eyes closed, say out loud: "I ask my body to accept this new truth or healing on a cellular level." Hold this position until you know that you don't need to anymore. I now incorporate positive affirmations from Louise Hay's 101 Affirmations. For example, if I am releasing a memory about money, I would say, "I deserve an abundance of money and accept it now on a cellular level."

Your higher power is amazing and sometimes you will get a name for the emotion you are feeling. In my childhood, my emotions were not validated at all and I felt mostly anger, fear and humiliation. I don't always have a name for what I am feeling.

Ask for guidance. Your higher power wants you to create and live a great life, a blessed life.

Be very careful not to release too much at once. These are your coping mechanisms that you have developed to protect yourself, and you have used them to live your life so far. It can be a little bit traumatic to release too much at once because it is important you give yourself time to be comfortable with each healing. Some beliefs and behaviors that you heal, you will need to figure out how to replace new beliefs and behaviors. Be prepared to go through the grieving process for releasing some of the deep-rooted issues – the process is different for everyone. Anger, crying, and blaming are common.

Afterwards, let go of the blame and take back your power. Remember what I said in the forgiveness chapter: let yourself off the hook. You have done the best that you have been able to do. Now that you know better, you will do better.

I have not shared everything I have healed in this book. I wanted to share the major ones with you to inspire you. The healing journey is very individual. At times it can be overwhelming, so DON'T DO IT ALONE!

I had to hit rock bottom and be stripped of my finances and home by trusting the wrong person in order to understand my truth. I believe that was because of the emotional depth of my abuse; the universe needed to hit me on the head with a 2 x 4 several times to wake me up. Not all of us need a 2 x 4!

My journey was amazing perfection. How incredibly timely and perfect each person was to mirror me back to myself, regardless of what happened during the time we were together. It was a choice for each of us to either hide the pain more or heal the pain. There are no regrets. Forgive me for my wrong doings, and I send love to each of you!

Since I have released and healed I have had so many incredible things happen. Serendipities! Last week, I was at a local pub, The Train Station, with a copy of this book to share with a friend. It was the first time I had printed it. I was sitting and waiting for her to show up when two guys walked up to me. The taller of the two said, "I think I know you."

I told him that I was advertising on the back of a bus for real estate and everyone thinks they know me. He said, "No, we actually met in Manhattan Beach, California, last October. You were taking a course on how to write a best seller in a weekend."

I was like, "Are you f****** kidding me!! Here is the book!!" It was mind boggling. His buddy was in shock, as we all were. Wow, that was crazy!! I often thought of him because I had changed the title several times since then and he had told me he was going to look for the book.

It took me two days to wrap my brain around what had happened.

We had met at a local pub in Manhattan Beach the first evening I was there. I sat beside him at the bar and noticed his suitcase and we started chatting. I asked him where he lived and he told me Vancouver, but his heart was in the Okanagan. His wife was going to school in Vancouver and that was where they were for now. Then there he was, the day I printed the first copy of my book!

I have noticed the flow of my life is becoming easier. The way I explain it to people is, "You know the story of how Moses put his rod in the sea, and the sea just parted? That's how my life is becoming now." Even though I have lived this amazing guided journey, I still get surprised how my spirit is guiding me. The universe is opening doors I never thought possible, just in this short amount of time. I find myself staying in that *place of grace* most of the time, without noticing myself doing it. That space that trusts and allows everything to unfold with the belief that it is exactly as it is meant to be. I wish that for everyone. I am excited to share the next part of my journey in the second book.

It has been a great joy to share this journey with you. Yes, there were some painful moments for me while writing this book. A few tears were shed, including right now – the difference is, these are happy tears. My prayer is that these words somehow reach whoever they need to and let them know that they are not alone and that they are understood.

There is a higher power that loves you and wants you to love yourself. I love you and wrote this book for you. I understand, I know you are worthy of healing, and you are important to this world. The way you heal is your story and your purpose. Share your purpose!

Blessings!

Connect with Me

Please reach out to me I would love to hear from you! I do small speaking engagements. I also offer support and coaching.

31dimesfromheaven@gmail.com
Facebook: Sara McClellan

A portion of the proceeds from each book sold will be donated to both the Elizabeth Society and the Woman's Shelter in memory of Kristen Porrelli.

Made in the USA
Middletown, DE
21 March 2022

62994402R00068